At the Feet
of
Rabbi Gamaliel

At the Feet
of
Rabbi Gamaliel

*Rabbinic Influence
in Paul's Teachings*

Rabbi Dr. David Friedman

Lederer Books
A division of
Messianic Jewish Publishers
Clarksville, MD 21029

2019   6

ISBN-13: 978-1-936716-75-3

Library of Congress Control Number: 2013952870
Printed in the United States of America

Lederer Books
A division of
Messianic Jewish Publishers
6120 Day Long Lane
Clarksville, MD 21029

Distributed by
Messianic Jewish Resources Int'l
Order line: (800) 410-7367
lederer@messianicjewish.net
www.messianicjewish.net

A NOTE FROM THE PUBLISHER

Please note the use and spelling of two words in the title of this book: Rabbi and Gamaliel. In the text, you'll find these changed to "Rabban" and "Gamliel." In the title, we use terms that are more familiar to our non-Jewish readers. Rabban is a term similar to that of Rabbi, but it represents a higher rank. The difference between Gamaliel and Gamliel is simply a difference in transliteration.

Foreword

I n this, his latest book, David Friedman brings together his vast
background as scholar, language expert, historian, and rabbi to
help the reader enter the world of the Shaliach Rav Shaul (Paul the
Apostle). Friedman focuses halakhic understandings and philosophical reasoning to establish a solid case for Rav Shaul's yeshi-
vah experience under Gamliel the Elder, grandson of Hillel. The
reader of this book comes away with a much deeper understanding
of Pauline thought and its nuanced elucidation of living a Jewish
life in Messianic Jewish community.

Friedman's approach progresses from reviewing the first and
second century Jewish writings, comparing these writings to
the letters of Paul, and then constructing rules for determining
authorship where Jewish writings do not carefully distinguish
between rabbis of the same name. Friedman goes on to review the
stories surrounding life in the School of Hillel, and then his focus
shifts to looking with care at Gamliel the Elder's household and
demonstrating the same values in the writings of Rav Shaul.

In this way, Friedman develops his thesis that Shaul grew
to maturity by sitting "at the feet of the Rabban," his mentor,
Rabban Gamliel. Friedman looks carefully at the earliest Jewish
sources (especially Pirkei Avot, the Traditions of the Fathers). He
juxtaposes select writings, notably those from the School of Hillel,

which were developed and handed down across generations from Hillel himself to his son Shimon, then to his grandson Gamliel I (or Gamliel the Elder), and then passed on personally to Shaul. When Friedman sets these Jewish writings alongside Shaul's own words from Pauline texts (1 Thess. 3:10; Gal. 6:1; Eph. 4:2; 1 Cor. 10:25-31; 2 Cor. 3:1-5; 10:3-5; 1 Tim. 2:1-2, 15; 3:2-6; 4:12; 6:10; 2 Tim. 2:24-25; Rom. 12:15; 13:3-7), it becomes obvious that Paul shared Gamliel's approach to Torah, Gamliel's worldview concerning Scripture and right relationship to God, and Gamliel's very personal father-to-student imprint for shaping his students as rabbis. Incredibly, Luke's summary corroborates this same understanding: "Then Paul said, 'I am a Jew, born in Tarsus in Cilicia, but brought up in this city, educated with strictness under Gamliel according to the law of our ancestors, and was zealous for God just as all of you are today" (Ac. 22:3).

Many of Friedman's eye-opening conclusions have implications for better understanding Scripture. Case in point: Paul did not "trash" his identity as Pharisee or Jewish person when coming to salvation in covenant with Yeshua (cf. Phil. 3:7-8). Rather, Paul's vocational dream changed from aspiring to be more like his mentor, Gamliel the Elder, a statesman, halakhic scholar, Sanhedrin judge or even Nasi (Vice President). The "changed" Paul aspired, instead, to be more like Yeshua, a humble bondservant, who poured out his life in sacrificial love for the well being of Yeshua's faithful. Ironically, the born-again Paul would do all that Gamliel had modeled for him. Paul would plant and care for communities, write responsa to settle issues, and even advise the powerful to treat their slaves as beloved members of their households.

All in all, one comes away from Friedman's "Sitting at the Rabban's Feet" with a newfound sense that Rav Shaul mentored Messianic Jewish communities, even as Rabban Gamliel had taught his students to mentor Jewish communities (Ac. 22:3). But there is one last twist to this story. Paul brought up his followers to sit at the feet of the greatest Rabbi of all (2 Cor. 3:18; Matt. 23:8).

Rabbi David Friedman has done us all a great favor by helping to sort out reader confusion over who actually mentored Rav Shaul. In so doing, the reader learns much about how Jewish communities develop leaders and mentor students to grow and mature. David's warm anecdotes, halakhic reasoning, and philosophical insights come together in a book that is readable and informative. The reader will be well rewarded for spending a few evenings sitting at the feet of Rabbi David Friedman.

—*Rabbi Jeff Feinberg, PhD*

Chapter One:

Shaul at the Rabban's feet

It is the opinion of this writer that the influence of *Rabban* Gamliel the Elder upon Shaul, his student, has neither been fully appreciated nor adequately analyzed. This is a difficult subject to write about due to the lack of material written *by* Rabban Gamliel or *about* Rabban Gamliel. Complicating the issue of understanding their relationship, there is an additional difficulty in identifying which Gamliel is written about in the Talmud in any given *aggadah*. There were at least three prominent men by that name. Neusner and Chilton succinctly stated the problem: "the problem of the historical Gamaliel proves complicated by the question: which Gamaliel, and to whom do otherwise-indeterminate Gamaliel-sayings and stories belong?".[1] Furthermore, while Shaul mentioned Gamliel as his teacher on a number of occasions, he did not go into any depth to define or explain this relationship. Yet there can be no doubt that the influence of the Rabban upon his student(s) would have been a large one, given the historical circumstances surrounding the life of Shaul.

The lack of ancient, first-hand textual evidence that clearly explains the relationship between Shaul and Gamliel makes it difficult to know the extent of personal contact between them. We do not know how often Shaul personally heard Gamliel teach, nor how close their relationship had been. Though Shaul indicates that he was a personal student of Gamliel, that is, in his teacher's close circle, there is almost no evidence to corroborate this fact. Thus, we have to work around this problem by examining the existing evidence to deduce Gamliel's influence upon Shaul.

We cannot be 100% sure that when Rabban Gamliel is referred to in Talmud texts that we have reference to Gamliel the Elder (a.k.a Gamliel I, or more formally Rabban Gamliel ben Shimon). Questions arise if we may not have reference to his grandson, also named Rabban Gamliel (a.k.a. Gamliel II, and more formally *also* Rabban Gamliel ben Shimon). In spite of this historical problem, I have identified certain Talmudic passages as descriptive of Rabban Gamliel the Elder, Shaul's teacher. Granted that some scholars may disagree with my identification of such passages with him, I have carried out my identification as part of my assessment of "which Gamliel was this Gamliel?" Most ancient texts contain some uncertainties, and the ones upon which I rely to carry out this study are no exceptions. Some commentators have a perspective that I share, stated in these words: "Tradition probably contains many sayings of Gamliel I, which are erroneously ascribed to his grandson of the same name"[2]. Yadin recognizes the same problem: "The identification of every occurrence of Rabban Gamliel with Rabban Gamliel II is a late convention that has been imposed upon a number of sages who carry that name. Though the identification may hold in many instances, there is no justification for making it into an inviolable rule. Moreover, even if the *Mekhilta* 'intends' to represent Rabban Gamliel II—and this cannot be ascertained—the actual historical setting reflected in the exchange remains an open question" [3].

Yadin attempts to identify "which Gamliel is which" through analyzing the given historical setting. For example, he notes: "the historical setting of Rabban Gamliel II's *floruit* (flourishing), from shortly after the destruction of the Second Temple, through the revolt of the Jewish Diaspora, to shortly before the Bar Kokhba revolt, does not lend itself to cultured exchanges between a Jewish leader and a pagan philosopher"[4]. I attempt to do the same with my limited knowledge of the given historical settings. Sometimes the text of Talmud helps us identify which Gamliel is which, as in this example, through the specific wording: "Ema Shalom, the wife of R. Eliezer, who was also a sister of R. Gamaliel *the Second*, encountered a philosopher in her neighborhood who was a judge[5], italics mine). The following piece of Gemara also specifically identifies which Gamliel is being referred to:

> R. Gamaliel said to the sages: "Thus it has been handed down to me from the house of my grandfather (Gamliel the Elder) that sometimes the new moon appears elongated and sometimes diminished."[6]

Here we clearly know that we are working with a quote from Gamliel II of Yavneh. Similarly, we read:

> Said R. Gamaliel to them: "Thus it has been handed down to me by tradition, from *the house of my grandfather*, the consecration of the moon cannot take place at a period less than twenty-nine and a half days, two-thirds and .0052."[7] (italics mine)

The Mishnah only specifically designates which Gamliel was Gamliel on rare occasions. The following narrates how Gamliel the Elder used to determine the new moon sighting:

> There was a large court in Jerusalem called Beth Ya'azeq, where all the witnesses met, and where they were examined by the Beth Din. Great feasts were made there for (the witnesses) in order to induce them to come frequently. At first they did not stir from there all day (on the Sabbath), till *R. Gamaliel, the elder*, ordained that they might go two thousand ells on every side; and not only these

(witnesses) but also a midwife, going to perform her professional duties, and those who go to assist others in case of conflagration, or against an attack of robbers, or in case of flood, or (of rescuing people) from the ruins (of a fallen building) are considered (for the time being) as inhabitants of that place, and may go (thence on the Sabbath) two thousand ells on every side. How were the witnesses examined? The first pair was examined first. The elder was introduced first, and they said to him: Tell us in what form thou sawest the moon; was it before or behind the sun? Was it to the north or the south (of the sun)? What was its elevation on the horizon? Towards which side was its inclination? What was the width of its disk? If he answered before the sun, his evidence was worthless.[8] (italics mine)

Another narrative identifies the Gamliel mentioned as Gamliel the Elder:

Said R. Jose: It happened that Aba 'Halafta went to R. Gamaliel the Great in Tiberias, who sat at the table of Johanan the Nazuph (also called Ben Nazuph), and held in his hand the book of Job in Aramaic, which he was reading. Said Aba 'Halafta to R. Gamaliel: "I remember having at one time come to *thy grandfather R. Gamaliel, who stood on the steps of the corridor of the Temple* when a Book of Job in Aramaic was brought to him. He told the mason to take the book and immure it underneath the stairway." Whereupon the later R. Gamaliel also ordered the book he was reading to be immured.[9] (italics mine)

8

A simple calculation, based on the language used, identifies Gamliel the Elder ("thy grandfather . . . corridor of the Temple") in contradistinction to Gamliel II. My working assumption is that when Gamliel is mentioned along with Rabbis Yehoshua, Yosi, Shimon, Yonatan, Eliezer, Elazar or Akiva, I presume him to be Gamliel II of Yavneh, the grandson of Gamliel the Elder. When Gamliel's name is mentioned alongside any Temple function, or with reference to the city of Jerusalem, I identify him as Gamliel the Elder. There is much 'in-between,' i.e. mentioning of Gamliel that is not well identified, thus falling into the problematic area that has been discussed. Future scholarship will have to more accurately fix the dating of our quoted texts and the assigning of them to the appropriate Gamliel.

Shaul came to the Land of Israel in the role of an "oleh," an immigrant, to engage in studies to become a Pharisaic judge in the Sanhedrin, or possibly to become a renowned Torah teacher. He describes his immigration:

> I am a Jew, born in Tarsus of Cilicia, but brought up in this city (Jerusalem). Under Gamaliel I was thoroughly trained in the law of our fathers and was just as zealous for God as any of you are today. . . . The religious leaders all know the way I have lived ever since I was a child, from the beginning of my life in my own country, and also in Jerusalem." (Acts 22:3,5, CJB with one change by the author)

He explains his sectarian allegiance within 1st century Judaism:

> [I had] b'rit-milah on the eighth day, an Isra'eli by birth, from the tribe of Binyamin, a Hebrew-speaker, with Hebrew-speaking parents, in regard to the Torah, a Parush, in regard to zeal, a persecutor of the Messianic Community, in regard to the righteousness demanded by legalism, blameless . . . (Phil. 3:5-8, CJB)

9

In another section of his letter to the Romans, Shaul picks up other positive aspects of being Jewish in stating:

> They [the people of Isra'el] were made God's children, the *Sh'khinah* has been with them, the covenants are theirs, likewise the giving of the *Torah*, the Temple service and the promises; the Patriarchs are theirs; and from them, as far as his physical descent is concerned, came the Messiah, who is over all. Praised be *ADONAI* forever! *Amen.* (Romans 9:4-5, CJB)

Let us understand that Shaul was on the "fast track" to becoming a sage and Sanhedrin judge. His self-description depicts himself as passionate for the Torah and the traditions of the fathers, typical for an aspiring Pharisee: ". . . trained at the feet of Gamli'el in every detail of the Torah of our forefathers. I was a zealot for God, as all of you are today" (Acts 22:3, CJB). In Philippians, we read Shaul addressing his particular vocational path:

> But the things that used to be advantages for me, I have, because of the Messiah, come to consider a disadvantage. Not only that, but I consider everything a disadvantage in comparison with the supreme value of knowing the Messiah Yeshua as my Lord. It was because of him that I gave up everything and regard it all as garbage, in order to gain the Messiah. (Phil. 3:7-8, CJB)

It is necessary to address a misassumption that is often taken as fact regarding Shaul. When he states *zemian* "disadvantage (twice)" and *skubalon* "garbage" in the above quoted section from Philippians, he is not saying that being Jewish or that being a Pharisee was somehow a "disadvantage" to him, or to be considered as nothing but "garbage." If he is taken or interpreted as meaning so, then he would have been contradicting other statements that he made, such as: "Then what advantage has the Jew?

What is the value of being circumcised? Much in every way! In the first place, the Jews were entrusted with the very words of God. (Romans 3:1-2, CJB).

I paraphrase Philippians 3:7-8 in these words: "Due to its greater value to me, I abandoned my vocational aspirations and have taken up another 'calling,' with a prophetic message, as messenger to the nations, to draw them to the One True G-d." Shaul gave up his vocational track and dream—to become a sage akin to Hillel or Gamliel, as well as that of being a Sanhedrin judge who would be active in legislating *halakha*—but not his lifelong identification of being Jewish or a Pharisee.

It is difficult to know the exact age of Shaul when he came to Israel to study. But, given the customs of the time, it is logical to assume that he was between the ages of 13 and 17. One Talmudic text, highlighting teachings of Pharisaic scholars (some of whom were Shaul's contemporaries) gives us some insight into this question:

> He [Yehuda ben Teima, approx. either 130 C.E., or 220 C.E.] taught: A five year old goes to study the Written Torah; a ten year old goes to study the Mishna; a thirteen year old is ready to keep the mitzvot; a fifteen year old goes to study the Gemara; an eighteen year old gets married; a twenty year old begins his career; a thirty year old becomes strong; a forty year old has understanding; a fifty year old gives counsel; a sixty year old is an elder; a seventy year old has white hair [and thus is deserving of respect]; an eighty year old is supernaturally strong; a ninety year old is stooped over; and a one hundred year old is nearly dead, and passed on from this world. (Avot 5.25, author's translation)

Tractate Avot of the Talmud, quoted above, offers us the highlighted teachings of Pharisaic scholars, some of whom were from Shaul's time period. Some of the language used in ben Teima's quote above could indicate a later date than the 1st century. Using words such as "Mishna" and "Gemara" is an indication that we may have a teaching from a later time period. Nevertheless, when ben Teima gave this teaching, the Pharisees' ideal life cycle for a Jewish man had been set forth. Jewish tradition assigns ben Teima's lifetime to be during the late 1st or early 2nd century. Certainly this would be a close enough time period to that of Shaul, making it plausible that the two would share a similar Jewish ethos, including the concept of what constitutes an ideal lifestyle. Such renders ben Teima's teaching relevant to our study.

Assuming that Shaul's family placed him in an educational tract consistent with ben Teima's ideal life cycle, we see from ben Teima's teaching that Shaul would have immigrated to Israel to study under Rabban Gamliel sometime around age 13 to 15. In fact, such an immigration to Israel for the purpose of advancing one's studies is consistent with a teaching that was fundamental to Rabban Gamliel: "Find a rabbi for yourself . . ." (Avot 1.16, author's translation). Another good translation renders this teaching: "Provide yourself with a teacher" (Avot 1.16, Shechem organization).

Pharisaic thought on the ideal situation for a student, is relayed again in Tractate Avot:

> Yosi ben Yoezer from Tsereda and Yosi ben Yohanan from Jerusalem received the tradition from them: Yosi ben Yoezer from Tsereda taught: Let your home be a house where the sages gather, and cling to the dust of their feet, and so thirstily drink their words. (Avot 1.4, author's translation)

Further defining this term, "To 'cover yourself with the dust of their feet' means to sit at the feet of a sage, to humbly learn from him or, if one wanted to travel with a sage to learn Torah from him, one literally had to *cover oneself with the dust of his feet"* (taken from http://www.razzberrypress.com/jewish_phrases_and_idioms.html). Rabbi Taragin provides further understanding on this idiom:

> (The) literal meaning of this phrase is based upon an outdated method of Torah study. Several commentators to the Mishna allude to the fact that students would sit at the feet of their Rebbe when studying Torah. This arrangement was adopted because of a lack of suitable seating or, and perhaps additionally to, demonstrate reverence toward Torah teachers. Either way, by encouraging us to sit as the feet of teachers, the Mishna is effectively urging us to study Torah with them. (taken from: http://vbm-torah.org/archive/avot/19avot.htm)

Taragin adds the insight of *Avot de-Rabbi Natan* to this Mishna (Pirke Avot 1.4):

> 'When a student enters the Beit Midrash he should not convince himself that he has no need of a Rebbe. He should sit in front of one. Consequently, he should not sit on an even level with the Rebbe, but in front of him *on the ground* accepting his words with fear and awe as Torah was initially delivered from Har Sinai.' It is quite easy to see how *Avot de-Rabbi Natan* saw in this image a metaphor for the humility which a student should sense in the presence of his Rebbe. As a parallel Gemara in *Megilla* (21a) asserts, the awe should be patterned after, and also stems from, the initial delivery of Torah at Sinai. By recreating this sensation during every learning experience, the talmid retains the sense of Torah's Divine origins. (taken from: http://vbm-torah.org/archive/avot/19avot.htm)

Furthermore, Luke records Shaul's description of his experience with Gamliel:

> I am a Jew, born in Tarsus of Cilicia, but brought up in this city and trained at the feet of Gamli'el in every detail of the Torah of our forefathers. I was a zealot for God, as all of you are today. (Acts 22:3, CJB). The Greek text states: εγω ειμι ανηρ Ἰουδαιος, γεγεννεμενος εν Ταρσω της Κιλικιας ανατεθραμμενος δε εν τη πολει ταυτη, παρα τους ποδας Γαμαλιηλ πεπαιδευμενος κατα ακριβειαν του πατρωου νομου ζηλωτης υπαρχων του θεου καθως παντες υμεις εστε σημερον; ego eimi aner Ioudaios, gegennemenos en Tarso tes Kilikias, anatethrammenos de en te polei taute, para tous podas Gamaliel pepaideumenos kata akribeian tou patroou nomou, Zelotes huparkon tou Theou kathos pantes umeis este semeron.

It is of note that the very Jewish idiom "at the feet of" is used in this verse, even though it is preserved for us in Koine. This is the language and imagery of Pharisaic literature. Thus, Shaul notes that he was educated "para tous podas Gamaliel . . ." literally, "at the feet of (Rabban) Gamliel," in keeping with the Pharsaic injunction to "cling to the dust of their [the Pharisaic sages'] feet, and drink their words with thirst" (Avot 1.4, author's translation,[10]). Rabbi Taragin comments on the phrase "drink their words with thirst" as follows: "[The] phrase is also easily understood, in urging the intake of Torah knowledge, just as a thirsty person would drink refreshing water" (taken from http://vbm-torah.org/archive/avot/19avot.htm).

The idiom used for "brought up in this city" (that is, in Jerusalem) is *anatethrammenos de en te polei taute* (Acts 22:3). This phrase reveals to us some of the influence of Rabban Gamliel upon Shaul. The Greek word used in this verse, "anatethrammenos," is usually translated as "brought up." This gives us an interesting insight.

Shaul was a native of Tarsus in the area of Cilicia (in modern day southeastern Turkey). Yet it is interesting that he stated that he was "brought up" in Jerusalem. Did his parents not bring him up in Tarsus? By "brought up," it would appear that Luke is telling us that Shaul considered his learning under Gamliel's tutelage as primary to his identity, his personal history, and to his *raison d'etre*. This was so much so that Shaul considered his time of advanced learning with Gamliel as his definition of what it means to be "brought up." A more specific Greek word could have been used to relay the idea of "educated" (as opposed to the more general "brought up") if this had been this verse's sole intent. It was during that period of time in Jerusalem as Gamliel's student that Shaul learned to understand and interpret the Torah according to the Pharisees' tradition. It was there that he was schooled in the halakhic viewpoints of the great sage Hillel, and consequently in those of Rabban Gamliel, the *Nasi* of the Sanhedrin.

Thus, Shaul's own *emphasis* on reaching maturity involves his time and experience in Jerusalem, not particularly his years of upbringing in Tarsus. Additionally, it is useful to keep this perspective in mind while considering Shaul's shift from the main Pharisaic "fold" towards the Jerusalem group of Messianic Jewish leaders (including James, Peter, and John). In line with Taragin's thought, he remarkably retains a respectful tone towards Gamliel and other Pharisees throughout his life. This fact indicates that Shaul never purposely "split-off" from the Pharisees due to any feud, theological or political. There is no concrete evidence for him having abandoned the Pharisee's midst in any enigmatic, angry or dispute-oriented fashion. In his personal identification, it appears that Shaul never divorced himself from Pharisaic party membership. Again, Luke informs us: "But knowing that one part of the *Sanhedrin* consisted of *Tz'dukim* and the other of *P'rushim*, Sha'ul shouted, "Brothers, I myself am a *Parush* and the son of *P'rushim;* and it is concerning the hope of the resurrection of the dead that I am being tried!" (Acts 23:6, CJB, italics mine).

Once again, Shaul's family made study possible for him and enabled him to "sit at the feet of the rabbi and drink in his words thirstily." If Shaul refers to his biological father in this verse ("the son of *a Pharisee*"), then his family may have sent him to Israel as an act and an extension of their family's piety. Shaul stated: "I myself am a *Parush* and the son of *P'rushim*" (Acts 23:6, CJB). However, if the phrase "son of a Pharisee" is a 1st century idiom that strongly emphasizes his sectarian allegiance more than his patristic genealogy, then the focus would be on his strong identification as a Pharisee. It is also of note that Shaul's nephew probably followed his example and came to Israel to study under similar circumstances to those of his uncle. In so doing, the wider family was acting true to their religious-based convictions: "But the son of Sha'ul's sister got wind of the planned ambush, and he went into the barracks and told Sha'ul (Acts 23:16, CJB).

In Acts 23:17, the Greek word used to describe Shaul's nephew, "neanian," typically refers to a youth who is beyond puberty but not yet marriage-eligible.[11] This would match up well with the typical age of an advanced yeshiva student from that time period. In the first century Jewish world, the ages of 13 to 15 would match up well with this description. If Shaul's nephew was following in Shaul's proverbial footsteps, then estimating Shaul's age of immigration to Israel as having been between 13 to 15 would appear accurate. The placing of Shaul into Gamliel's "yeshiva" or study academy (termed "Bet Hillel" in its identification in rabbinic literature) was a continuation of Shaul's background and family life—it does not a reflect his choosing a new direction for his life. Shaul stated the following in an impassioned talk to King Agrippa:

> So then! All the religious leaders know how I lived my life from my youth on, both in my own country and in Yerushalayim. They have known me for a long time; and if they are willing, they can testify that I have followed the strictest party in our

> religion—that is, I have lived as a Parush. (Acts
> 26:4-5, CJB, with one change by the author)

This verse highlights the point that an influential number of
contemporary religious leaders knew Shaul personally, or at least
had become familiar with his reputation. Presumably, the term
"religious leaders" refers to the Sanhedrin, the Pharisees and the
High Priest's family. Josephus informs us that there were 6,000
Pharisee party members in the late 2nd Temple period. If that
was an accurate figure, we can account for the situation where a
number of Pharisees whom Shaul addresses in chapter 26 may not
have known him personally, and may never have met him, all the
more so because he had been abroad for good stretches of time in
the years preceding the Acts chapter 21-26 events.

On the other hand, Shaul notes, "They have known me for
a long time." He may have been known by a good number of
religious authorities in Jerusalem, and may have maintained a
strong and positive reputation with his former classmates.

As Shaul appeals to the religious leaders' ability to give a
legal witness to his personal history, he displays not only personal
familiarity with them but such an appeal also reflects his good
relationships with them, even after his allegiance to Yeshua as the
promised Messiah. Luke records the giving of an oral testimony by
Shaul to the Sanhedrin in Jerusalem, and its results, in these words:

> But knowing that one part of the Sanhedrin consisted
> of Tz'dukim and the other of P'rushim, Sha'ul
> shouted, 'Brothers, I myself am a Parush and the
> son of P'rushim; and it is concerning the hope of
> the resurrection of the dead that I am being tried!'
> When he said this, an argument arose between the
> P'rushim and the Tz'dukim, and the crowd was
> divided. For the Tz'dukim deny the resurrection
> and the existence of angels and spirits; whereas the

P'rushim acknowledge both. So there was a great uproar, with some of the Torah-teachers who were on the side of the P'rushim standing up and joining in—'We don't find anything wrong with this man; and if a spirit or an angel spoke to him, what of it?' (Acts 23:6-9, CJB)

In the first century, Bet Hillel (which includes the students of Hillel, of Shimon [Hillel's son], of Gamliel the Elder, and of Yohanan ben Zakkai), were known for studying the following "subject" matters:

It was taught that Rabbi Yohanan ben Zakkai studied the Written Torah, Mishnah, Gemara, halakha, aggadah, small details of the Torah, small details of the scribes, inferences, analogies, the calendar, gematria, the talk of angels, the talk of spiritual beings, and the talk of palm trees, stories about fullers and foxes, and other important and not so important matters. (Sukkah 28a, author's translation)

The three first sages mentioned of Bet Hillel lived in a time span from approximately 1 C.E. to 50 C.E. In spite of the fact that it may be debated how much of what later became the Mishnah was available for study in the early and mid-first century, leave alone the "Gemara," the above was the study matter of Bet Hillel's students. It is logical to assume that Shaul would have been learned in a good number of these same subject areas as a result of his studies under Gamliel. It is possible to see such learning evidenced in his writings. This would have made Shaul an advanced student of the interpretations and approach to life that Hillel, Shimon ben Hillel, and Gamliel held. Hillel is credited with being the father of 1st century Pharisaic thought, which was continued on and developed by his son Shimon, and by Hillel's grandson, Gamliel.

In this way, the "dynastic" tradition of Torah interpretation was passed down, and included Shaul among its students and adherents. It is revealing that Shaul, during his oral testimony of Acts 23, states that: "*Ego pharisais eimi*," literally, I *am* (a present tense verb in the Greek text) a Pharisee." It is unclear whether he was specifically stating that he continued to adhere to Pharisaic halakhic practice, or whether he meant by these words to remind his audience of his personal alignment with the Pharisaic bloc of the Sanhedrin. Certainly both of these possibilities are credible, and I would assert probable. Proving Shaul's continued strict adherence to Pharisaic practice is taken up in my book *They Loved the Torah* to which I refer the reader. Additionally, the Roman governor Festus' evaluation of Shaul looms interesting:

> [The Roman governor] Festus shouted at the top of his voice, 'Sha'ul, you're out of your mind! *So much learning* is driving you crazy!' But Sha'ul said, 'No, I am not 'crazy,' Festus, your Excellency; on the contrary, I am speaking words of truth and sanity.' (Acts 26:24-25, CJB, italics mine)

Shaul impressed at least this one Roman official with the extent of his Torah-based learning.[12]

The events recorded in Acts chapter 23-26 occur in approximately 60 C.E., an estimated two to three years prior to Shaul's death in Rome. Thus towards the end of his life, Shaul is recorded, by Luke, as stating, "I am a Pharisee," *ego Pharisais eimi*, in the *present* tense. I discuss in *They Loved the Torah* that Shaul always lived as a strictly Torah observant Jew, keeping Torah and Jewish customs in the manner prescribed by Bet Hillel of the Pharisees. A remark made by Shaul in Acts 28:17 attests to such:

> . . . ego andres adelphoi, ouden enantion poiesas to lao he tois ethesi tois patroois desmios etz Ierusolumon paredothen eis tas keiras ton Romaion. . . . Brothers, although I have done

nothing against either our people or the traditions of our fathers, I was made a prisoner in Yerushalayim and handed over to the Romans. (Acts 28:17, CJB)

Luke informs us that Shaul had never taken any adverse actions towards Pharisaic tradition (i.e. "the traditions of our fathers"), not even politically, that is, against the welfare of the nation (e.g. fomenting a rebellion). Finally, in the Acts narrative, Shaul mentions, "my hope in the resurrection of the dead" (23:6). These words cemented and emphasized his Pharisaic mindset, linking Shaul to both Bet Hillel and Bet Shammai in the discourse of Acts 23. At this point in Shaul's life, Luke again depicts him to be a "confessing" Pharisee.

We can conclude then, by Shaul's own words above, that he came from a Torah-loving family allied to the Pharisees. He was then sent to study in Jerusalem to become a learned, Land of Israel-based scholar and/or judge. As he studied under Rabban Gamliel, in the tradition of Bet Hillel, Shaul became an advanced student of the interpretations and life-approach in the same school of thought as Hillel, Shimon ben Hillel, and Gamliel. Hillel is credited with being the father of 1st century Pharisaic thought, which was continued on and developed by his son, Shimon, and grandson, Gamliel. In this way, the "dynastic" tradition of Torah interpretation was passed down, and included Shaul among its students and adherents. He was headed for becoming a Sanhedrin judge and teacher par excellence of the Torah when he took another vocational path: that of serving a prophetic message to the nations surrounding Israel. His life as a messenger of Israel's promised Messiah should be understood in this compelling light. The connections made above show us that Shaul's self-identity, his historical recounting and his theological milieu all were connected to Gamliel, to whom he continued to speak of respectfully after becoming a follower of Yeshua.

Chapter Two:

The Avot and Shaul

Many of the sages quoted in Tractate Pirke Avot of the Talmud lived just prior to, during, or just after the lifetime of Shaul. Their teachings would be the milieu in which Shaul lived and was educated. Their values were those that were instilled into Shaul. Thus, in comparing some of their teachings to those of Shaul, we can see the valid intersection of content, ways of thought, and methods of expressing such. By doing this, we can better understand the world of Pharisaic teaching, capture some of the main emphases of Bet Hillel (including Gamliel the Elder) and, thus, understand Shaul's thought within such context. Perhaps through Pirke Avot's verses we have ways to identify the influence of Bet Hillel in Shaul's life. Therefore, this chapter examines a chosen set of teachings from Pirke Avot, and makes any obvious, above-mentioned connections between Shaul's teachings and those of his contemporaries.

I value Pirke Avot as a compendium of highlighted teachings of selected Tannaim. These summary teachings were chosen by the students of the given sages to be remembered as their overall perspectives on learning and living Torah. Pirke Avot primarily contains non-halakhic teachings that give us a view of overall values and principles held by the Pharisaic rabbis who are quoted therein.

Pirke Avot 1.7 notes: "Nitai from Arbel taught: Get far away from an evil neighbor; don't cling to an evil person; and do not fret about (the timing of) Divine retribution" (author's translation).

Similarly, Shaul teaches about behavior towards wicked persons and their actions, albeit he most often does so by writing in his responsa about actual situations: "By rejecting conscience, some have made shipwreck of their trust; among them are Hymenaeus and Alexander. I have turned them over to the Adversary, so that they will learn not to insult God" (1 Tim. 1:19-20, CJB). And again:

> Alexander the metalworker did me a great deal of harm. The Lord will repay him for what he has done. You too should be on your guard against him, because he strongly opposed our message (2 Tim. 4:14-15, NIV) . . . but keep away from every form of evil. (1 Thess. 5:22, CJB)

By using the verb "philasso" in 2 Timothy 4:15, Shaul would appear to be instructing Timothy, his ally and student, to carefully stay away from Alexander and his dangerous influences. In doing this, Shaul adheres to what Nitai had taught, some years prior to Shaul's life.[1] Of course, one could argue that Shaul was simply following the instructions of Proverbs 1:10-19, by advocating the distancing of oneself from persons intent on causing problems:

> My son, if Torah transgressors entice you, don't go! If they say: 'Come with us, we'll ambush and shed blood; we'll hide, and freely get away with our actions. We'll swallow them alive, like She'ol; and whole, like a victim of a sinkhole. We'll find all sorts of valuables, and we'll fill our houses with plunder. Share our fate! We'll have one pocket for all of us.' My son, don't go on the road with them! Prevent your feet from their paths! Since their

feet are set on doing evil; they hurry up and run to commit bloodshed. Because a net gets spread out right in front of all the birds, in vain. But they set ambushes to shed their own blood; they hide in wait for their own lives. That is the fate of every greedy robber; their very lives are taken away (Proverbs 1:10-19, author's translation).

There is every reason to see Nitai's teaching as consistent with, and perhaps an extrapolation on, this Proverbs text. In fact, this very same theme is repeatedly emphasized throughout biblical texts. In writing his exhortations to avoid wrongdoers, one could simply say that Shaul was wisely avoiding his enemies' influence, without any encouragement to do so through the oral teachings of Nitai. Though that is a logical point, nevertheless, the conceptual connection between Nitai's teaching and Shaul's writing and behavior remains true.

It is probable that Shaul advocates similar actions in his more theoretical teaching given in 2 Corinthians:

Do not yoke yourselves together in a team with unbelievers. For how can righteousness and lawlessness be partners? What fellowship does light have with darkness? What harmony can there be between the Messiah and B'liya'al? What does a believer have in common with an unbeliever? What agreement can there be between the temple of God and idols? (2 Cor. 6:14-16a, CJB).

Here, Shaul strikes some interesting images in these verses. "Lawlessness" (*anomia*) would certainly refer to a lifestyle that first-century Jews were encouraged to wholly avoid. This would accord with the instructions of Nitai in Avot 1.7.

The Greek word "anomia" was understood as referring to a life that is in contradiction to the instructions and morals of the Written Torah. The contrast between "Messiah and B'liya'al [Belial]" uses strong language to depict a strong contrast between two persons: one being "good" [Messiah], the other being evil [Belial]. Thus, Shaul's admonition is to avoid persons who live an evil, Torah-despising lifestyle. Suffice it to say that a God-fearing person would necessarily have to avoid some of the known lifestyle options then available in the ancient seafaring port of Corinth—including the practice of idolatry, alcohol addiction, and male prostitution.[2]

Furthermore, Shaul contrasts the "Temple of God" to "idols." Again, this image evokes avoidance as a tactic because any God-fearing Jew would necessarily have to keep away from Hellenist-cult idols. We can then see that Shaul's instructions to avoid partnering with "darkness, idols" and "Belial" certainly agrees with the call of Nitai to "distance oneself from an evil neighbor." Granted that in Shaul's statements here, perhaps individuals are not being thought of, but communities and their lifestyles. Nevertheless, both Shaul and Nitai, in Avot 1, advocate similar behavior while facing this challenge.

In sum, there is a nice parallel between these two teachers regarding behavior towards evil and wicked ways. Shaul's teaching is thoroughly consistent with that of his earlier pro-Pharisaic colleague, Nitai.[3]

Another intersection between Shaul and his contemporaries is found in the lifestyle choices they did support. Various sages taught: "Shemaiah and Avtalyon received (teaching) from them. Shemaiah taught: Love work, shun strong-arming others, and do not draw close to the government" (Avot 1.10, author's translation). The word used here for "work" is *hamela'kah*, in contrast to the word *avodah*. *Avodah* is a more commonly used word that can mean either physical labor or a profession—it can mean "worship," perhaps through gathering in a *minyan* and prayer. However, *hamela'kah* is used here and means physical labor, i.e. a profession, which combined with Torah study was

24

considered the proper lifestyle choice in ancient Israel. Gamliel is quoted in one teaching upon this very subject:

> Rabban Gamliel said, 'Whoever has a (profession) craft, to what may he be compared? To a vineyard that is surrounded by a fence and a to a furrow that is surrounded by a border.'

The following teaching, circa. mid-3rd century, reflects similar sentiment:

> Rabban Gamliel, the son of Rabbi Yehudah the Nasi taught: Torah study is good with an (accompanying) occupation; the efforts from both of them causes transgressions (of Torah) to be forgotten; and all Torah study that isn't accompanied by an occupation will end in leading to transgression of Torah. (Avot 2.2, author's translation)

Shaul also encourages such a combination in the following verses to his students in the Greek city of Thessalonika:

> We were not idle when we were among you. We did not accept anyone's food without paying; on the contrary, we labored and toiled, day and night, working so as not to be a burden to any of you. It was not that we hadn't the right to be supported, but so that we could make ourselves an example to imitate. For even when we were with you, we gave you this command: if someone won't work, he shouldn't eat! We hear that some of you are leading a life of idleness—not busy working, just busybodies! We command such people—and in union with the Lord Yeshua the Messiah we urge them—to settle down, get to work, and earn their own living. (2 Thess. 3:7b-12, CJB)

Clearly, Shaul advocates the lifestyle that Gamliel, Shemaiah and Avtalyon also advocated, where a profession was combined with Torah study and its application. Shaul insists that even as their teacher, he and his entourage did not rely upon his students to support them. Instead, they carried out the dictum of Shemaiah and Avtalyon (and later of Rabban Gamliel ben Yehudah), to support themselves. As an example of a proper lifestyle, Shaul studied and taught the Torah while also working and earning his own finances. This is in keeping with (and even went beyond) the Pharisaic teaching on this matter. Further, Shaul taught: ". . . when we were with you, this is what we instructed you: that if anyone is unwilling to work, neither will he eat (2 Thess. 3:10, author's translation).

Although we do not know specifically who was unwilling to earn a wage, such an attitude was considered unworthy of a student of Yeshua. To be considered a part of the community, with its unspoken benefits and responsibilities, one was expected to attempt to earn his own keep. Shaul's Pharisaic background no doubt influenced the formation of his attitude as expressed here, and he spreads it among the Gentile students of the Jewish Messiah, as well, in this letter of instruction.

Regarding another issue, the sage Shemaiah, and Shaul, both advocated the use of gentle persuasion in lieu of using more forceful means in relationships with others. In their roles as leaders, logically both men had situations that required them to judge situations and "put their foot down." They both advocate doing so in a gentle and humble way: "*shun strong arming others*" (Shemaiah in Avot 1.10; it being taken for granted by the author that those he teaches are in a position to be able to 'strong arm' others); "*set him right in a spirit of humility* (Shaul). Furthermore, Shaul taught, "Brothers, suppose someone is caught doing something wrong. You who have [God's] Spirit should set him right, but in a spirit of humility, keeping an eye on yourselves so that you won't be tempted too" (Gal. 6:1, CJB).

At this point in history, Gamliel may have been the *Nasi*, and thus his opinion and advice would have carried weight. He was known for being flexible, innovative and even compassionate in his halakhic decisions. Chapter Four of this work discusses his reputation in these areas. Please refer to it, especially the three incidences where Gamliel is questioned by his students for practicing a flexible, compassionate halakha that was innovative and suited to the concept of *hora'at hasha'ah* (a later developed principle in which halakha is practiced to best fit a pressure or emergency situation). One example will suffice to illustrate my point:

> He bathed on the first night after his wife died. His students questioned him: 'Our honored rabbi, you taught us that it is forbidden for a mourner to bathe.' He answered them: 'I'm not like most people; I am elderly and frail." (M. Berakot 2:6, BT, author's translation)

Gamliel displays a compassionate flexibility in his orthopraxy here, even though the given halakhic practice concerns himself. In this instance, it was accepted halakhic practice to refrain from bathing when in the initial period of mourning. Yet while in mourning, Gamliel bathed, citing to his inquisitive students that he was too frail to desist from a warm bath. Given that he was no doubt elderly, and emotionally distraught by the loss of his wife, it was compassionate to permit himself to bathe in order to assuage some of his discomfort. This practice applied halakha in a more flexible manner than the accepted standard in this difficult situation.

Gamliel is known for interpreting halakha in such a way as to aid widows, as well as showing compassion to the residents around Jerusalem in his role of setting the monthly calendar. Here are relevant texts:

> Rabbi Akiva said: When I went down to Nehardea to declare a leap year, I met Nehemiah of Bet D'li

who said to me; I heard that in the Land of Israel no one, with the exception of Rabbi Yehudah ben Baba, permits a [widowed] woman to remarry, based on the evidence of one witness. I (R. Nehemiah of Bet D'li) have this tradition from Rabban Gamliel the Elder, that a [married] woman is allowed to remarry, based on the evidence of one witness. And when I came to relate the conversation in the presence of Rabban Gamliel, he rejoiced at my information exclaiming, 'We have found a colleague for Rabbi Yehudah ben Baba!' As a result of this, Rabban Gamliel remembered that some men were once killed at Tel Arza, and that Rabban Gamliel the Elder had allowed their wives to remarry, based on the evidence of one witness. And the law was established that [a woman] is allowed to remarry on the evidence of one witness and on the evidence of a witness who states that he has heard the report from another witness, [or] from [the testimony of] a slave, from [the testimony of] a woman or from [the testimony of] a maidservant. (Yevamot 16.7; taken from: http://www.emishnah. com/Nashim_Vol_1/Yev16.pdf)

Likewise, Shaul should be known for interpreting halakhic practice the same way. Much of his work involved applying the Torah and its principles to the community life of his Gentile students. I view his responsa to the Corinthians in this light. In doing so, he necessarily needed a certain amount of these very same qualities— flexibility, innovation and compassion—while remaining true to the halakha enacted by the Messianic Jewish Sanhedrin as relayed in Acts chapter 15. The prior halakhic work of his teacher Gamliel could have played an influential role in molding Shaul's approaches to flexibility, innovation, and compassion in applying the Torah's principles and commandments to his communities. There is no hard and fast evidence to prove this point, but once again, it is very logical to assume.

Another point of intersection is demonstrated in how Shaul decides to teach non-Jewish believers in the Jewish Messiah on how they ought to behave in relation to eating with pagans. The Messianic Jewish Sanhedrin laid the groundwork for answering this question as relayed in Acts chapter 15:

> [Regarding] the Gentiles who are turning to God . . . we should write them a letter telling them to abstain from things polluted by idols, from fornication, from what is strangled and from blood. For from the earliest times, Moshe has had in every city those who proclaim him, with his words being read in the synagogues every Shabbat. (Acts 15:19-21, CJB)

Yet how would applying this piece of halakha look in Corinth? This was the question that Shaul had to deal with as their rabbinic authority (and their direct, appointed connection to the early Jerusalem-based Messianic Jewish community). The idea of interpreting the Torah and halakhic practice with a bent towards *darkey no'am* is presented in the Messianic Jewish Sanhedrin's decision quoted above. *Darkey no'am* encompasses a perspective on how to apply the Torah so that it can be kept without posing discouraging difficulties; i.e. it is the rabbinic authorities' attempt to make the Torah's commandments accessible to all followers. Given the propensity of Gamliel and Bet Hillel to share this same perspective, it is not surprising that we see Shaul do this in his "responsa" as well.

> Eat whatever is sold in the meat market without raising questions of conscience, for the earth and everything in it belong to the Lord. If some unbeliever invites you to a meal, and you want

to go, eat whatever is put in front of you without raising questions of conscience. But if someone says to you, "This meat was offered as a sacrifice," then don't eat it, out of consideration for the person who pointed it out and also for conscience's sake — however, I don't mean your conscience but that of the other person. You say, "Why should my freedom be determined by someone else's conscience? If I participate with thankfulness, why am I criticized over something for which I myself bless God?" Well, whatever you do, whether it's eating or drinking or anything else, do it all so as to bring glory to God.. (1 Cor. 10:25-31, CJB)

In his halakhic instruction, Shaul displays some flexibility. Instead of coming with a hard and fast directive, he attempts to teach his students the principle by which to apply halakhic practice to a given question (as well as giving his directive!).

One of Hillel's sayings is comparable, on another point, to material in Shaul's writings. "He [Hillel] would teach: 'Whoever promotes his reputation, loses his reputation'" (Avot 1.13a, author's translation). The idea of "advancing one's name" (*negad shema*) means to promote one's self and one's reputation; to attempt to increase one's influence. The Pharisees of the first century taught against making such efforts. As a student of first century Pharisaic teaching, Shaul acted in accordance with Hillel's teaching, by indeed refusing to advance his own reputation. He wrote to his students in Corinth:

Are we starting to recommend ourselves again? Or do we, like some, need letters of recommendation either to you or from you? You yourselves are our letter of recommendation, written on our hearts, known and read by everyone.

You make it clear that you are a letter from the
Messiah placed in our care, written not with ink
but by the Spirit of the living God, not on stone
tablets but on human hearts. Such is the confidence
we have through the Messiah toward God. It is
not that we are competent in ourselves to count
anything as having come from us; on the contrary,
our competence is from God. (2 Cor. 3:1-5, CJB)

In this rather touching part of his letter, Shaul lets his contacts in
Corinth know that there was no need for him to use his personal
accomplishments, his education, or his Pharisaic background to
create respect among them for him. Neither did he ask for written
recommendations from any other accomplished or honored persons
in order to authorize his teachings among them. He appeals to *their
already established relationship* as proof of his authority. Shaul
gives honor to God for any accomplishments that he was able to
affect among the Corinthians, stating: "our competence comes
from God" (2 Cor. 3:5, NIV). The Greek word *ikanotos* is used
here and can mean "competence" or, perhaps is better understood
as "qualification." Thus Shaul's qualifications to bear authority as
the rabbi to the Corinthians was simply through his past contact
with them, and via the teaching, supervision, and advising gifts
that God had granted to him.

Gamliel, as the Nasi, wrote to Jewish communities, both in
and out of Israel, concerning accepted halakhic practice and to
update those communities on decisions that were made by the
Great Sanhedrin. The Talmud records this in stating:

For it has been taught: It once happened that Rabban
Gamaliel was sitting on a step on the Temple-hill
and the well known Scribe Johanan was standing
before him while three cut sheets were lying before
him. 'Take one sheet,' he said, 'and write an epistle
to our brethren in Upper Galilee and to those in

Lower Galilee, saying: "May your peace be great! We beg to inform you that the time of 'removal' has arrived for setting aside [the tithe] from the olive heaps." Take another sheet, and write to our brethren of the South, "May your peace be great! We beg to inform you that the time of 'removal' has arrived for setting aside the tithe from the corn sheaves." And take the third and write to our brethren the Exiles in Babylon and to those in Media, and to all the other exiled [sons] of Israel, saying: "May your peace be great for ever! We beg to inform you that the doves are still tender and the lambs still too young and that the crops are not yet ripe. It seems advisable to me and to my colleagues to add thirty days to this year.'" (Sanhedrin 11b, Soncino translation, taken from: http://www.come-and-hear.com/sanhedrin/ sanhedrin_11.html#PARTb)

This section of Talmud records that Gamliel sent letters to Jewish communities; to Galilee, to the "south," and then to Diaspora communities in Babylon and in Media. These letters instructed the community leaders on how to deal with tithes as well as informing them of the decision to declare a leap year.

Similarly, Shaul engaged in writing to his communities of students also on issues of accepted halakhic practice, including updates on halakhic decisions that were made by the Messianic Jewish Sanhedrin in Jerusalem. His letters to the Corinthians, Philippians, Thessalonians, and to Timothy could be defined as such letters. Although one cannot say that Shaul engaged in letter-writing to the Diaspora *because* Gamliel did the same, we must note that the two teachers did engage in this similar activity in order to communicate halakhic decisions to their students and constituents.

Shaul was careful about the character traits of the men whom he installed in congregational leadership roles. In his relationship with his young (Jewish) student Timothy, Shaul stressed the qualities that Timothy needed to cultivate and express in his role as a leader:

> Here is a statement you can trust: anyone aspiring to be a congregation leader is seeking worthwhile work. A congregation leader must be above reproach, he must be faithful to his wife, temperate, self-controlled, orderly, hospitable and able to teach. He must not drink excessively or get into fights; rather, he must be kind and gentle. He must not be a lover of money. He must manage his own household well, having children who obey him with all proper respect; for if a man can't manage his own household, how will he be able to care for God's Messianic Community? He must not be a new believer, because he might become puffed up with pride and thus fall under the same judgment as did the Adversary. . . . Don't let anyone look down on you because of your youth; on the contrary, set the believers an example in your speech, behavior, love, trust and purity. (1 Tim. 3:2-6, 4:12 CJB)

Two character traits stand out as parallels between Hillel's teaching and Shaul's admonitions to Timothy. One is the presence of timidity, shyness or bashfulness in the life of a serious Torah student. The other is a tendency to invest too much time, effort, and resources in worldly pursuits, namely, earning money: "For the love of money is a root of all the evils; because of this craving, some people have wandered away from the faith and pierced themselves to the heart with many pains" (1 Tim. 6:10, CJB). Let us examine Avot 2 to see some further likenesses.

> Be careful with the government, for they befriend
> a person only for their own needs. They seem to
> be friends when it is beneficial for them, but they
> do not help a person in his time of trouble. . . .
> Hillel would teach: Do not isolate yourself from
> the community. A shy person cannot study, a short-
> tempered person cannot teach, nor can anyone who
> engages in a lot of business grow wise. *(Avot 2.3,
> 4b, 6, author's translation)*

Hillel taught: *"velo' habayshan lamed"* (a shy person cannot study [Torah]). Hillel teaches here that it is necessary to be a bold student: assertive and inquisitive. The stories of Hillel's life illustrate such an attitude. He is recorded as almost having frozen to death, sitting on a rooftop in winter in the Jerusalem snow and cold, to hear the lessons of the *Nasi* in the *Bet Midrash*. This illustrates the meaning of a "bold student," one possessed of a hunger that takes risks. This is not only in keeping with Pharisaic custom, but with general Jewish practice throughout our history. I am reminded of the story of Rabbi Aryeh Levin's life, recorded in his biography by Simcha Raz. In it, Raz chronicles how Levin as a youth left home, spending cold nights on hard benches in the bet midrash, sleeping there, sometimes going hungry; in order to study Torah[4]. To learn the Torah, one is encouraged to ask many questions, to be aggressive in taking a text apart and learning the nuances of every word and every possible angle of understanding a portion of Torah. I am reminded of my first day as a student in *bet midrash*. After an intense, hours-long study of one mishna of the Talmud, the supervising rabbi, an elderly scholar, came over to my partner and myself. He asked me: "So, how was your study session? Friedman, did you study our mishna well?" "Yes, rabbi, we looked at every word in it, read the commentaries, and discussed it thoroughly. I really enjoyed it." "Good. Have any questions for me?" I thought for a minute, and I responded, "No, I think we answered every question I had right here in our discussion." "Ummm, I see," the rabbi said, and walked away. Suddenly, he whirled around and pounded his fist on our table. He pointed his index finger at me and said sternly, "Questions, questions, questions, without questions, how are you going to learn!?"

Shaul encourages Timothy to be bold, and not shy. In particular, as a leader and Torah teacher, Timothy was encouraged to be the outstanding example of how to live and behave. This matches what Hillel taught his students, although Hillel may have been referring to the study of the texts of Torah in particular.[5] Rabbi Meir is quoted in Pirke Avot with a similar teaching: "Rabbi Meir taught: Don't look at the tin can, but instead at what is inside of it. There is a new tin can that is full of old things, and old (cans) that have nothing new in them" (Pirke Avot 4.20, author's translation).

Rabbi Meir's teaching is meant to emphasize that youth is not necessarily a block to scholarship. The legend of Rabbi Meir is that he was considered too young to merit studying as a student of Rabbi Akiva. However, overnight his hair turned white, conferring dignity and maturity to him. Thus he was considered to be worthy of studying the Torah. Similarly, Shaul did not consider Timothy's young age to be any issue that should prevent him from effective leadership in his community. In this matter, Shaul agrees with Rabbi Meir, who followed him by some 100 years.

Additionally, the rabbinic teaching of praying for political peace is upheld by both Shaul and many sages: "Rabbi Hanina, a deputy officer of the kohens, taught: Be in prayer for the peace of the government; if not for fear (of it), a man would swallow up his neighbor's life" (Avot 3.2).

The quoted sage is Hanina ben Teradion (2nd century), who lived during the Hadrianic years, and was killed by the Roman government (approximately 133 A.D.). Hanina would have seen himself in the line of Pharisaic teaching, tradition, ethics, and halakhic practice, in spite of the fact that he was apparently a priest (kohen). He was the father-in-law of the famed Rabbi Meir. Rabbi

Hanina's teaching is quite interesting in that although he believed in cooperating with the secular government, he was eventually murdered by them for taking part in a forbidden activity (i.e. teaching the Torah during

Hadrian's harsh anti-Jewish persecutions). Although Rabbi Hanina tried to live peacefully given the political constraints of the time, and taught his students to do so, his Roman overlords were not able to do so with him. Similarly, Shaul instructed the following to his Jewish student Timothy:

> First of all, then, I counsel that petitions, prayers, intercessions and thanksgivings be made for all human beings, including kings and all in positions of prominence; so that we may lead quiet and peaceful lives, being godly and upright in everything. (1 Tim. 2:1-2, CJB)

Further, Shaul wrote to another set of his students at Rome itself:

> For rulers are no terror to good conduct, but to bad. Would you like to be unafraid of the person in authority? Then simply do what is good, and you will win his approval; for he is God's servant, there for your benefit. But if you do what is wrong, be afraid! Because it is not for nothing that he holds the power of the sword; for he is God's servant, there as an avenger to punish wrongdoers. Another reason to obey, besides fear of punishment, is for the sake of conscience. This is also why you pay taxes; for the authorities are God's public officials, constantly attending to these duties. Pay everyone what he is owed: if you owe the tax-collector, pay your taxes; if you owe the revenue-collector, pay revenue; if you owe someone respect, pay him respect; if you owe someone honor, pay him honor. (Rom. 13:3-7,CJB)

Similar to Hanina, Shaul taught his students to honor the government that rules in their area, and to pay their taxes. This also follows the teaching of his Messiah (cf. Mt. 22.15-21). In an eerie and sad similarity to Hanina, Shaul was also murdered by the Roman government, as well by an emperor's edict (Nero). Yet, both teachers saw a positive role that government plays in maintaining social order and peace, protecting its citizens against bullying and criminal elements within society.

Other Pharisees are noted for addressing perspectives on government-Jewish community relations. One of them was Yohanan ben Zakkai, who was a famous sage during the First Roman War. The following *aggadah* concerning this sage's political position illustrates the fact that some prominent Pharisees did not believe in rebellion against the Romans, for whatever reason: whether it was a tendency for self-preservation, holding pacifist tendencies, or believing that God would bring Israel through the Roman domination without the need for bloodshed.

> The Zealot guards were then in the city. The Rabbis said to them: Let us go out and make peace with them [the Romans]. They would not let them, but on the contrary said, Let us go out and fight them. The Rabbis said: You will not succeed. They then rose up and burnt the stores of wheat and barley so that a famine ensued… Abba Sikra, the head of the biryoni in Jerusalem, was the son of the sister of Rabban Johanan b. Zakkai. [The latter] sent to him saying, Come to visit me privately. When he came he said to him, How long are you going to carry on in this way and kill all the people with starvation? He replied: What can I do? If I say a word to them, they will kill me. He said: Devise some plan for me to escape. …He said to him: Pretend to be ill, and let everyone come to inquire about you. Bring

something evil smelling and put it by you so that they will say you are dead. Let then your disciples get under your bed…He did so, and R. Eliezer went under the bier from one side and R. Joshua from the other…They opened a town gate for him and he got out. When he reached the Romans he said, Peace to you, O king, peace to you, O king. He [Vespasian] said: Your life is forfeit on two counts, one because I am not a king and you call me king, and again, if I am a king, why did you not come to me before now? He replied: As for your saying that you are not a king in truth you are a king, since if you were not a king Jerusalem would not be delivered into your hand…As for your question, why if you are a king, I did not come to you till now, the answer is that the Zealot guards among us did not let me. (Gittin 56a, Soncino Edition, with two vocabulary changes by the author).

Rabban Yohanan and his students escaped the coming conflagration in the city, putting their fate into the hands of the Roman attackers. There is evidence in this text to believe that Yohanan viewed Vespasian as fulfilling scriptural precedent. As a Pharisee and student of Gamliel the Elder, Rabban Yohanan's position was one of not bearing arms against the government in this instance, even if such government was oppressive in nature. He apparently bargained successfully with the Roman authorities for the right to start a new Sanhedrin in Yavneh, for the life of his colleague Shimon ben Gamliel, and for a physician to attend to another beloved teacher, Rabbi Tsadok: "You [Yohanan] can, however, make a request of me [Vespasian] and I will grant it. He said to him: Give me Yavneh and its Wise Men, and the family chain of Rabban Gamliel, and physicians to heal R. Zadok." (Gittin 56a, Soncino edition).

There is no exact parallel in Shaul's writings regarding this event, as it is doubtful that he was alive by the outbreak of the war. Yohanan's position is consistent with the more politically moderate stance of the Pharisees (as opposed to the support of revolution given by the Zealots and the Sicarii). This is not to say that the Pharisees had any innate sympathy towards the Roman occupiers. As Flusser has noted: "At that time most Jews hated the occupying Roman power of Rome. The party known as the Zealots believed that armed struggle against Rome was divinely ordained . . . one of the 12 apostles had been a zealot at one time."[6]

Perhaps Shaul followed the overall Bet Hillel sympathy of finding non-violent ways to endure the Roman occupation, and survive beyond it. In addition, he may have adhered to his understanding of his Messiah on this very issue: "Jesus was no supporter of revolt against them" (Rome,[7]). Shaul noted:

> For although we do live in the world, we do not wage war in a worldly way; because the weapons we use to wage war are not worldly. On the contrary, they have God's power for demolishing strongholds. We demolish arguments and every arrogance that raises itself up against the knowledge of God; we take every thought captive and make it obey the Messiah. (2 Cor. 10:3-5, CJB)

This is a comment, perhaps in contrast, to those advocating waging a flesh and blood war against the Romans, who occupied large areas across the entire Middle East.

Shaul makes it clear that he and his students are engaged in a spiritual type of war that does not involve earthly armies; their area of warfare was in the arena of ideas and philosophies, fought with non-physical weapons. In taking this position, Shaul de facto follows his mentors, the Pharisees of Bet Hillel, while also following the approach of his Messiah, Yeshua.

Both Yohanan and Shaul displayed a penchant for giving due honor to the given government, and neither participated in armed revolt, though both had the opportunity to do such. Shaul taught his students to pray for the government, and as citizens to meet their social obligations. Yohanan taught his students to refrain from revolt against the government; to continue living as Torah faithful Jews, and in this way perhaps "outlast" the government's hold on the area. At any rate, both teachers displayed a similar respect for governmental authority, and distaste for bearing arms. We could surmise that they reasoned that the nation would not survive warfare against the Empire, but that God's promises would endure forever (and thus so would the people of Israel). But that point is conjecture.

Yohanan's decision is portrayed in a positive light by the compilers of the Gemara, in contrast to the Zealots, who are portrayed as cruel and makers of trouble for their own people, the validity of their political complaints aside. In fact, Yohanan cites the blockage of the city by the Zealots as the reason that he did not come to Vespasian for clemency before he did so: "(If) I did not come to you till now, the answer is that the biryoni (Zealot guards) among us did not let me" (Gittin 56a, Soncino edition).

On Yohanan's stategy, it has been written:

> (Yohanan) wisely foresaw that Jerusalem was doomed and understood the need to transplant the center of Torah scholarship to another location, to ensure the survival of Torah study after Jerusalem's destruction. He devised a plan that would allow him to leave Jerusalem, despite the Zealots' blockade. He feigned death so that he could be carried out of the city. His disciples carried the coffin out of the city's walls, and Rabbi Yochanan proceeded directly to Vespasian's tent. (taken from: http:// www.chabad.org/library/article_cdo/aid/953564/ jewish/Rabbi-Yochanans-Request.htm)

Instead of his attitude being considered strange for the Jewish world, I would contend that Shaul was following the line of thought espoused by most of Bet Hillel, including Rabban Gamliel the Elder. Historically speaking, this would have been founded in the textual message of Israel's role to the world (cf. Ex. 19.5-6, Deut. 4.5-8). Shaul's approach toward Roman occupation can be easily seen as a strong stream of first century Jewish thought. This thought retained a role for Israel to be the proverbial "light to the world," spreading God's Torah along with Israel's messiah. Such an attitude would have to put the political problems of that era in a secondary position. In other words, Shaul's belief about what the messiah was meant to do and his effect in the world was less centered on political methods and implications, and more focused on teaching the entire world about Israel's God and His ways.

Another interesting area of comparison between the Tannaim and Shaul concerns the positive value of having many teachers: "Ben Zoma taught: 'Who is wise? The one who learns from every person, as it is written: 'I have been educated by all my teachers . . .'" (Avot 4.1, referring to Ps.119.99; author's translation).

In stating this, Shimon Ben Zoma (early 2nd century) hit upon an important idea: that every student can learn from any number of given teachers. A student, therefore, is not solely restricted to having a single teacher. A Jewish student of the Torah in the first century, while loyal to his immediate teaching rabbi, would also have considered his biological father, his mother, his study partners, older and more experienced students, and affiliated rabbis as his teachers. Thus, for Shaul learned approaches to various matters from Bet Hillel, from Gamliel directly, and from Yeshua through the oral tradition of Yeshua's immediate students. He also learned by "direct revelation" (cf. Galatians 2.1-2a). This was not a pedagogic rarity. Having numerous or multiple teachers of Torah was a reality; there was not one teacher par excellence over all Israel; fact, a spirited rivalry existed between Galilean and Judean Torah teachers. This situation mirrored what the author of

Proverbs wrote: "Plans fall apart when they have no foundation; but with many advisors, it [the plans] will come about (Prov. 15.22, author's translation). A student could have one main teacher and supervisor, such as Gamliel, but was certainly able to learn from a variety of other sources and persons.

The subject of argumentation in pursuit of understanding the Torah is an area of Pharisaic influence upon Shaul. Let us examine relevant texts:

> Any (halakhic) dispute that is for the sake of Heaven will last; one that is not for the sake of Heaven will not last. What (halakhic) dispute is for the sake of Heaven? The dispute(s) between Hillel and Shammai. Which dispute is not for the sake of Heaven? The dispute of Korach and all his ilk. (Avot 5.17, author's translation).

Perhaps this teaching would be the proper background by which to understand the dispute between Shaul and Shimon (Kefa). Some of my students have found the evidence of this dispute to be upsetting, that two of the early leading students of Yeshua would have a serious difference of opinion between them:

> Furthermore, when Kefa came to Antioch, I opposed him publicly, because he was clearly in the wrong. For prior to the arrival of certain people from the community headed by Ya'akov, he had been eating with the Gentile believers; but when they came, he withdrew and separated himself, because he was afraid of the faction who favored circumcising Gentile believers. And the other Jewish believers became hypocrites along with him, so that even Bar-nabba was led astray by their hypocrisy. But when I saw that they were not walking a straight path, keeping in line with the truth of the Good News, I said to Kefa, right in front of everyone, 'If you, who

are a Jew, live like a Goy and not like a Jew, why are you forcing the Goyim to live like Jews? We are Jews by birth, not so-called "Goyishe sinners"; even so, we have come to realize that a person is not declared righteous by God on the ground of his legalistic observance of Torah commands, but through the Messiah Yeshua's trusting faithfulness. Therefore, we too have put our trust in Messiah Yeshua and become faithful to him, in order that we might be declared righteous on the ground of the Messiah's trusting faithfulness and not on the ground of our legalistic observance of Torah commands. For on the ground of legalistic observance of Torah commands, no one will be declared righteous. But if, in seeking to be declared righteous by God through our union with the Messiah, we ourselves are indeed found to be sinners, then is the Messiah an aider and abettor of sin? Heaven forbid! Indeed, if I build up again the legalistic bondage which I destroyed, I really do make myself a transgressor.' (Gal. 2:12-18, CJB)

Additionally, Shaul had another dispute with his friend Barnabas, so severe that it caused them to temporarily part company:

After some time, Sha'ul said to Bar-nabba, 'Let's go back and visit the brothers in all the towns where we proclaimed the message about the Lord, and see how they're doing.' Now Bar-nabba wanted to take with them Yochanan, the one called Mark. But Sha'ul thought it would be unwise to take this man with them, since he had gone off and left them in Pamphylia to do the work by themselves. There was such sharp disagreement over this that they separated from each other, with Bar-nabba taking Mark and sailing off to Cyprus. (Acts 15:36-39, CJB)

43

However, when we understand that passionate argumentation about Torah related issues was a part of the Jewish world, the meaning of such disputes can take its proper place. Sharp differences of halakhic opinion among Torah authorities are to be considered a normal state of affairs in the Jewish world. This holds true for the ancient world, as well as for the modern world. Thus, when we look at the differences between Shaul and Shimon, on one hand, and Shaul and Barnabas on the other hand, we may be looking at similar situations to that of what occurred between the adherents of Bet Hillel and Bet Shammai. There were differences being held due to differing approaches, both philosophical and halakhic. Yet in ancient Israel when such differences appeared, it was almost always the obligation of the holders of the variant opinions to give way to the decision of the majority (i.e. to the vote of the Great Sanhedrin).

The problem concerning halakhically-based issues that Shaul brings up in Galatians is one that he chalks up to the temporary hypocrisy of his Messianic Jewish Sanhedrin colleague, Shimon:

> Furthermore, when Kefa came to Antioch, I opposed him publicly, because he was clearly in the wrong. For . . . he had been eating with the Gentile believers; but . . . he withdrew and separated himself, because he was afraid of the faction who favored circumcising Gentile believers. And the other Jewish believers became hypocrites along with him, so that even Bar-nabba was led astray by their hypocrisy. But when I saw that they were not walking a straight path, keeping in line with the truth of the Good News, I said to Kefa, right in front of everyone, 'If you, who are a Jew, live like a Goy and not like a Jew, why are you forcing the Goyim to live like Jews?' (Gal. 2:11-14, CJB)

What we have here is a dispute between the two leaders on how to enforce the Messianic Jewish Sanhedrin decisions recorded in Acts

15. Shaul, in attempting to uphold these decisions, passionately confronts Shimon, whom he believed to be straying from those decisions that they had all agreed to uphold. After discussing the matter between them—semi-publicly and passionately—the correct, Jerusalem community approved practice was restored in Galatia. Or simply put, Shaul's opinion ruled the day, and Shimon apparently reneged on his former opinion or practice, and submitted to Shaul's understanding.

Whether Shaul and Shimon's issue was more than a one-sided dispute is not made clear, but I will logically assume that Shimon discussed the issue with Shaul, as well, and did not just disappear into the background. Let us note that this was not a personal or character issue between the two Messianic Jewish authorities. It was centered on the correct practice of halakha. This dispute did not result in any final split between the two of them. This would have been rare in the ancient Jewish world, as passionate disputes, confrontations, and discussions concerning the correct practice of the mitzvot of the Torah were all considered a regular part of life. So it is no surprise that later in his writings, Shimon writes to his students about Shaul in brotherly, allied, and friendly terms:

> And think of our Lord's patience as deliverance, just as our dear brother Sha'ul also wrote you, following the wisdom God gave him. Indeed, he speaks about these things in all his letters. They contain some things that are hard to understand, things which the uninstructed and unstable distort, to their own destruction, as they do the other Scriptures. (2 Peter 3:15-16, CJB)

It is clear that Shimon retained his positive and collegial relationship with Shaul after the recorded halakhic dispute in Antioch. If we view Shaul's dispute with Shimon as being "for the sake of Heaven," it makes sense. Avot 5.20 defines what this term means:

Any halakhic dispute that is *for the sake of Heaven,* will endure in the end. But if it is not for the sake of Heaven, [it] will not endure in the end. Which is the halakhic dispute that is for the sake of Heaven? The dispute between Hillel and Shammai. And not for the sake of Heaven? The dispute of Korach and all of his allies. (Avot 5.20, author's translation, italics mine)

These arguments, "for the sake of Heaven," should not be seen as overly personal in nature. The argumentations are not meant to pit one person or rabbi's personality against that of another. Neither should these disputes be seen as the cause of any final split between the involved parties. Bet Hillel and Bet Shammai continued to relate to one another as colleagues, in spite of 316 cited halakhic differences of interpretation and practice between them. In the case of Bet Hillel and Bet Shammai, we are told that their students intermarried with those of the other 'school':

Although Beth Shammai and Beth Hillel are in disagreement on the questions of rivals, sisters, an old bill of divorce, a doubtfully married woman, a woman whom her husband had divorced and who stayed with him over the night in an inn, money, valuables, a perutah and the value of a perutah, Beth Shammai did not, nevertheless, abstain from marrying women of the families of Beth Hillel, nor did Beth Hillel refrain from marrying those of Beth Shammai. This is to teach you that they shewed love and friendship towards one another, thus putting into practice the Scriptural text, Love ye truth and peace. (Yevamot 14b, taken from: http://www.come-and-hear.com/yebamoth/ yebamoth_14.html#PARTb)

Bet Hillel on at least one occasion showed humility vis-à-vis Bet Shammai by acquiescing to the latter's halakhic decision:

> When one vintages [grapes] for the vat [to manufacture wine], Shammai maintains: It is made fit [to become unclean]; while Hillel ruled, It is not made fit. Said Hillel to Shammai: Why must one vintage [grapes] in purity, yet not gather [olives] in purity? If you provoke me, he replied, I will decree uncleanness in the case of olive gathering too. A sword was planted in the Beth Hamidrash and it was proclaimed, 'He who would enter, let him enter, but he who would depart, let him not depart!' And on that day Hillel sat submissive before Shammai, like one of the disciples. (Shabbat 17a, Soncino translation)

The later students of Bet Hillel apparently recorded this event, and gave their quite honest assessment of it: "It was as grievous to Israel as the day when the [golden] calf was made" (Shabbat 17a, Soncino translation).

In a similar manner, Shaul continued to relate to Shimon (and vice-versa) as a colleague, in spite of the noted difference between them. Of course, the viewpoint that we have is through the writing of Shaul and his scribe-historian, Luke. Thus we easily tend to read this dispute in a pro-Shaul manner; as a heated, one-sided, clearly "right" and "wrong" situation (Shaul being 'right'; Shimon being 'wrong'). I will add that however it is read, this type of dispute itself is within the framework of what we see occurring in the relationship between Bet Hillel and Bet Shammai, as well as in other 1st century Jewish relationships, within the world of Torah authorities. In this facet of his life, Shaul displays a likeness to the passionate argumentation that characterizes the "pilpul" (passionate, halakhic-centered arguing and reasoning) that was consistent with the serious application of the Torah that was such a large part of his world. (In fact, one of the disputes between Bet Hillel and Bet Shammai was so volatile, that it resulted in coming to blows.) I will comment more on this in the next chapter.

The dispute with Barnabas concerning Mark is relayed in one textual passage:

> After some time, Sha'ul said to Bar-nabba, 'Let's go back and visit the brothers in all the towns where we proclaimed the message about the Lord, and see how they're doing.' Now Bar-nabba wanted to take with them Yochanan, the one called Mark. But Sha'ul thought it would be unwise to take this man with them, since he had gone off and left them in Pamphylia to do the work by themselves. (Acts 15.36-39, CJB)

There was such sharp disagreement over this that they separated from each other with Bar-nabba taking Mark and sailing off to Cyprus.

In Avot 6.6, it is written:

> Torah is acquired by way of forty-eight means; they are: by study, by listening, by verbalizing, by understanding through one's mind, by education, through fear and awe, in humbleness, with joy, in purity, by paying attention to scholars, through study with colleagues, by debate with other students, studying alone, and through the study of the Written Torah, the Mishnah, by lessening one's business obligations and professional engagements; through limiting one's entertainment time, and limiting one's times of sleep; by less conversation time and less play-time; by being slow to anger, with a full effort, in the faith of the sages and by receiving sufferings; by not being self-promoting,

by being happy with one's state in life; and by being stringent in personal matters. By not being arrogant; by being loved, by loving HaShem, by loving His creation and righteousness; by loving what is correct, by loving reproof; through shunning honor, by not being proud of one's knowledge, and by not loving to reprove others. By carrying your friend's burdens, and judging him favorably, then helping him find the truth, and find peace; helping him concentrate on his learning through asking and answering, and listening then adding; by learning in order to teach and learning in order to do. By emulating one's teacher, through processing what one has learned, and by teaching in the name of one's teacher. You have learned: Everyone who teaches something in the name of his teacher, brings redemption to the world, as it is written, 'Esther spoke to the king in the name of Mordecai . . .' (Avot 6.6, author's translation)

Avot 6.6 was taught by Yehoshua ben Levi to his students in the 2nd century, as a response to the question, "How should we (that is, 'with what attitude') learn the Torah?" In spite of the time difference between himself and Shaul, the content of his teaching is not far removed from the philosophical bases of Shaul's thought. Shaul touched on nearly every aspect of what Yehoshua ben Levi stated above, as Shaul similarly instructed his students on how to learn and practice the Torah.

For a short comparison, Shaul and Yehoshua ben Levi both instruct their students on a number of similar themes, including the tremendous value of learning and teaching the Torah; the problems inherent in business pursuits; helping out with the burdens of others; boasting, and unseemly behavior for a Torah student and leader.

A few comparisons are noted directly below:

SHAUL's TEACHING (FROM HIS LETTERS)	YEHOSHUA'S TEACHING (from AVOT 6.6)
On business aspirations: 1 Timothy 3.3, 1 Timothy 6.10	"Lessening one's business obligations"
Bearing others' burdens: Romans 12.15, Galatians 6.2	"Carrying your friend's burdens"
Studying and teaching Torah: 2 Timothy 2.15	"through the study of the Written Torah"
Suffering for the Torah's sake: Romans 5.3	"by receiving sufferings"
Being humble: Ephesians 4.2, 2 Corinthians 3.1	"by not…self-promoting"
A leader possessing a moderate temper: 2 Timothy 2.24-25	"by being slow to anger"
Giving a great effort to learn & practice Torah: 2 Timothy 2.15	"with a full effort"

Shaul does follow many of the dictums and teachings that permeated the first century Pharisaic world, as well as that of the later sages, inheritors, and teachers of the Pharisaic tradition. Tractate Avot makes an interesting source for seeing Shaul as well within the Pharisaic tradition in a number of his responsa points. This should not be surprising; it is logical to assume that this should indeed be the case. He did not abandon the values that he was taught as a young man, *the very values that Gamliel would have taught to him*. The above mentioned parallels between Shaul's teaching and verses from Pirke Avot emphasize these logical connections.

Chapter Three:

Stories of Gamliel

From the *aggadot* of the Talmud, we have some wonderful and illustrative stories involving Gamliel that are preserved for us. As we analyze them, we are perhaps able to understand the student (Shaul) through the teaching and behavior of his rabbi (Gamliel the Elder). At the very least, we become more familiar with the overall personality of the Nasi and sage. Such familiarity can provide more insight as we analyze Shaul's teachings.

It is worthwhile to remember that Gamliel the Elder was the grandson of Hillel, and thus both Gamliel's lineage and education put him into the school of "Bet Hillel." That is, the interpretations of the Torah that Gamliel would have practiced and taught were within the legal framework of the movement that his grandfather pioneered.

This is in contradistinction to the interpretations and Torah observance of the other main Pharisaic tradition, termed "Bet Shammai." While our tradition identifies 316 differences in their respective halakhic practice, they did not represent distinct movements in Gamliel's lifetime. Still their differences were sharp enough to warrant comment in our tradition:

> But when the disciples of Shammai and Hillel, who
> had insufficiently studied increased [in number],

AT THE FEET OF RABBI GAMALIEL

> disputes multiplied in Israel, and the Torah
> became as two (Torahs). (Sanhedrin 88b, taken
> from: http://www.come-and-hear.com/sanhedrin/
> sanhedrin_88.html#PARTb)

In spite of many differences between the two schools, we have
at least one Talmudic passage where reconciliation and humility
are expressed between the two Pharisaic schools. In the following
passage, Bet Hillel is praised for its humility towards Bet Shammai:

> Since, however, both are the words of the living
> God, what was it that entitled Beth Hillel to have
> the halachah fixed in agreement with their rulings?
> Because they were kindly and modest, they studied
> their own rulings and those of Beth Shammai and
> were even so [humble] as to mention the actions
> of Beth Shammai before theirs (Eruvin 13b, taken
> from   http://halakhah.com/rst/moed/13a%20-%20
> Eruvin%20-%202a-26b.pdf).

Indeed, Gamliel was renowned for his humility: When Gamliel the
Elder died, the glory of the Torah ceased, and purity and abnegation
perished (Sotah 49a, Soncino Edition, with one change by the
author). Although the words used here in referring to Gamliel,
kavod ha-Torah, *taharah*, and *perishut*, do no specifically address
the matter of humility, when used together in a description, they
do paint such a picture.

Differences in interpretation and practice not withstanding,
their likenesses were surely more compelling. In rabbinic writings,
all recorded disputes were "for the sake of Heaven, that is, for the
purpose of deciding the best way to keep the Torah. Thus, to hold
these differences, ultimately, had a positive outcome and purpose:

> Every disputation that is for the purpose of Heaven
> will endure; if it is not (for the purpose of Heaven),

> it will not endure. Which type of disputation is for the purpose of Heaven? The type done by Hillel and Shammai. And which type is not for the purpose of Heaven? The disputation done by Korach and all of his associates (Pirke Avot 5.17, author's translation).

Perhaps we can view some of Shaul's halakhic disputes in a similar fashion. Shaul's sharp dispute with Shimon (Peter) can also be read in this light, as well as his dispute recorded in Acts chapter 15 with unidentified Messianic Jews: "Furthermore, when Kefa came to Antioch, I opposed him publicly, because he was clearly in the wrong.

And the other Jewish believers became hypocrites along with him, so that even Bar-nabba was led astray by their hypocrisy" (Gal. 2:11,13, CJB).

Shaul indicates that he had a sharp halakhic dispute with Shimon (Peter) concerning eating meals with non-Jews. In order to determine the truth of the Torah and how to live concretely by its instructions, Shaul entered into disputes with his colleagues that were "for the sake of Heaven." Certainly Shaul's participation in halakhic disputes in order to reach a positive outcome was a continuation of his education. As Bet Hillel engaged in this method of arriving at the truth of an halakhic issue, Shaul would have become familiar with this method through Bet Hillel and he would have carried this method over into his role as a Messianic Jew. Too often, commentaries on Shaul's disputations do not reflect this tradition or its role in Jewish education and Torah discourse but rather portray it as a sign of antagonism, in ability to work out differences, or a complete break of relationships.

Modern day athletes provide an apt analogy. Within athletic competitions on the field, the emotions, energy, and performance of the athlete are focused on the end goal. Yet when the game is over, most often athletes "leave it on the field." That is, they are able to fraternize with the opposing athletes, considering them as colleagues, not "enemies." That same situation exists in today's yeshivas (Jewish religious colleges). Torah disputation is done in a focused and energetic matter. Yet the disputants are always fellow students and colleagues, most often friends. They always are seeking to understand and apply the given point of disputation "for the sake of Heaven."

This is what Shaul did as he recorded in Galatians chapter 2 and as Luke recorded in Acts 15 and in Acts 22. Although it is easy to assess Luke's narratives as prejudicial to Shaul, nevertheless they can be valued as history, and Shaul's letter to Galatia is loosely akin to later rabbinic responsa, and is therefore valuable for its historic information.

Indeed, this tradition of engaging in sharp and vibrant "mahlokot" (disputations on Torah issues) remains in Jewish life today. I refer the reader to Zvi Lampel's "The Dynamics of Dispute" (see bibliography), a very interesting study on the purpose and makeup of halakhic disputations in Jewish history.

Let us examine a number of *aggadot* involving Rabban Gamliel and then analyze his character traits and *halakhic* perspective as much as possible from these periscopes.

> A groom is exempted from reciting the shema during the first night, until the end of Shabbat, if he had not yet performed the act of consummation. (Here is) an event involving Rabban Gamliel: he recited during the first night of his marriage. His students questioned him: 'Our honored rabbi, you taught us that a groom is exempted from reciting the shema (on the first night).' He answered them: 'I can't do according to what you say, to allow myself to renege on the Kingdom of Heaven, even for one hour.' (M. Berakot 2.5, BT, author's translation).

The halakhic ruling that Bet Hillel adhered to was that a groom who was just married did not have to appear in synagogue to pray (i.e. "recite the shema") on the evening of the day of his marriage. Rabban Gamliel, apparently, *did* attend synagogue on that evening to pray. When his students asked him why he was going against accepted opinion and the accepted custom on this matter, he responded that he would not stop his public prayers. We can glean from this that Rabban Gamliel was stricter with his own orthopraxy than he legally had to be. At least that is true in the given situation. We have an aforementioned situation, which occurred later in his life:

> He bathed on the first night after his wife died. His students questioned him: 'Our honored rabbi, you taught us that it is forbidden for a mourner to bathe.' He answered them: 'I'm not like most people; I am elderly and frail.'" (M. Berakot 2.6, BT, author's translation)

The accepted halakha was that a mourner did not bathe. When questioned by his students as to why he did bathe on the very evening after his wife had died, Gamliel responded that his physical condition (as an elderly person) merited taking a bath. He is telling us that his physical condition caused an exception to the accepted custom. He exhibits either a respect for the concept of "pikuah nefesh" or simply believed that someone in physical pain should take all means of alleviating that pain, even if it meant breaking one of the customs of mourning.[1] In this case, Gamliel is more lenient with himself, in contradistinction to being stricter with himself in the previously considered mishnah.

Another interesting story in the Mishnah relates:

> When his household servant Tabi died, he received condolences on his behalf. His students questioned him: 'Our honored rabbi, you taught us that one

doesn't receive condolences for servants!' He answered them: 'My servant Tabi wasn't like most servants. He was kosher.' (M. Berakot 2.7, BT, author's translation).

Again, Gamliel made a decision that went against accepted halakhic practice. In this mishnah, Gamliel received visitors who expressed their condolences at the death of his domestic servant, Tabi. According to most commentators, Tabi was not Jewish, and so there was no need for carrying out customary Jewish mourning practices. It appears that Gamliel wanted to honor his faithful servant, and so he posthumously showed respect for Tabi by keeping this Jewish mourning ritual.

Gamliel also taught about the value of learning and understanding the Torah:

> On the subject of disciples, Rabban Gamliel the Elder taught [there are] four kinds: the unclean fish, the clean fish, the fish from the Jordan River, and fish from the Great Sea. The unclean fish, how so? This is the poor son who studies Scripture, Mishnah, Halakhot and Aggadot but has no understanding. The clean fish, how so? This is the one who has studied and understood everything, and is the son of rich parents. The fish from the Jordan River, how so? This is the disciple of a sage who studies Scripture, Mishnah, Midrash, Halakhot and Aggadot but does not know how to answer. The fish from the Great Sea, how so? This is the disciple of a sage who studies Scripture, Mishnah, Midrash, Halakhot and Aggadot, and knows how to answer.[2]

Gamliel's emphasis above is on understanding the Torah, and acquiring the ability to teach it ("answer"). One would expect such a teaching from the Nasi of the Sanhedrin. As Gamliel's student, Shaul's ability to both understand and teach the Torah represents a success in the educational objectives of Gamliel (even though Gamliel may have disagreed with Shaul regarding the identification of Yeshua's role in the Jewish world). Again, I would encourage the student of Shaul to consider most of Shaul's writings as a rabbi writing about Torah in highly contextualized situations to his students.

Rabban Gamliel's death was considered a huge loss to ancient Israel, as relayed in the following two Talmudic teachings: "From the time Rabban Gamliel the Elder died, the glory of the Torah ceased, and purity and holiness died." (Sotah 49a, BT, author's translation).

> From the days of Moshe up until Rabban Gamliel, they did not study Torah unless they were standing up. From the time Rabban Gamliel died, sickness came upon the world, and they studied Torah in a sitting position. We also learned that when Rabban Gamliel died, the glory of the Torah was ceased. (Megillah 21a, BT, author's translation)

Gamliel's legacy, then, was one of having a great positive influence upon the Jewish world. His personal orthopraxy was praised, as was his holiness. Sotah 49a uses the Hebrew words "taharah" and "perishut" to describe what "died" when Rabban Gamliel did. "Taharah" refers to either spiritual or ritual purity. Perhaps here it entails both. "Perishut" entails living so as to affirm the sanctity of life.

CHAPTER FOUR:

Onesimus and Tabi

B oth Rabban Gamliel and Shaul had a special relationship with a household servant.[1] The institution of forced servitude and slavery were well known in the late Roman Republic: "At the height of the Empire in the mid second century AD, some have estimated that the total slave population may have approached 10 million people, or approximately 1/6 of the population as a whole".[2]

In the Jewish province of Judea, servitude was practiced, but not in the form of Jews being enslaved to other Jews. Professor Shmuel Safrai has written on the subject, and insists that slavery in that specific location at that time consisted of Gentile slaves working for Jewish families. Even then, the humanitarian treatment of Gentile servants was a known factor in that institution. In Gamliel's case, his personal servant appears to have been his domestic worker; in Shaul's case, the servant had belonged to one Philemon, and may have been a personal attendant of Shaul's for a given period of time. If that was the case, Onesimus performed volunteer service, with no compulsion involved.

Let us examine the scant textual evidence, and see if we can draw any conclusions about the attitude of Rabban Gamliel and his student Shaul regarding the treatment of servants.

Onesimus, once owned by Philemon, seems to have been a Gentile slave to a Gentile owner. Philemon was a resident of Colossae, whom perhaps Shaul befriended during his stay in the same region. It is not proven that Shaul ever spent time in Colossae itself, but he had been active in the region, thus it is logical to assume that he had met and taught Philemon during his travels. It is highly possible that Onesimus escaped from Philemon, and somehow was now living as a free man in Rome. The exchange in the letter from Shaul to Philemon would seem less possible if Onesimus had bought his freedom, which was a legal way to become a free man. Although we are totally in the dark concerning Onesimus' background, it is of note that Roman slaveholders particularly valued Greek slaves:

> Greeks were especially prized slaves for both their cultural refinement and education. Greeks with the ability to educate the Roman youth or with knowledge of medicine were expensive and highly sought after. By the late empire, the predominant house slaves in Rome came almost entirely from the east (and all its various ethnicities), as Western Europe and Africa were almost exclusively of citizen class.[3]

We can only venture educated guesses as to Onesimus' status. Onesimus may have been acquired by Philemon from anywhere in the Empire, and it is certainly possible that both Philemon and Onesimus were from an ethnic Greek background. Onesimus' Greek first name may well indicate a Hellenist background. Interestingly, the name Onesimus means "a profitable person," which seems to describe his value to Philemon. If Onesimus was an ethnic Greek slave, his disappearance may have been all the more troubling to Philemon in terms of loss of a quality servant. "Some slaves were well educated, especially those from Greece, and they would be used to teach the children of the house"[4] For, as mentioned above, Greek slaves were known for their "high quality" of work.

Catholic tradition explains that Onesimus committed a theft, and thus fled Colossae to escape punishment, ending up in Rome, where he met Shaul, through whom he became a believer in the Jewish Messiah Yeshua.[5] This can be surmised from the following verses: "And if he (Onesimus) has wronged you (Philemon) in any way or owes you anything, charge it to me. I, Sha'ul, write with my own hand. I will repay it" (Philemon 18-19, CJB). Other possibilities of the relationship exist, but are not clearly defined for us.

Another possibility is that Philemon may have sent his slave Onesimus to Rome to attend to Shaul, in order to help him. As we recall, Shaul was under house arrest in Rome under the rule of the volatile Emperor Nero. So it is possible that under Shaul's influence, Onesimus became a committed believer in the Messiah of Israel, thus giving rise to the possibility of a change of status (1). Whether this was an actual change in halakhic status (in Shaul's thought), or an appeal to enact a status from slave to free man, issued to Philemon's conscience, is not clear. It is even possible that Shaul personally paid for Onesimus' freedom (cf. vv. 18-19, "I Shaul say, I will repay it."). Thus, Shaul could have been appealing to Philemon to receive Onesimus now as a free man, and expect payment for such from Shaul (and thus Shaul carries out the role of a go'el, a monetary redeemer, even though this is only a known position from within a Jewish and Torah-based framework, cf. Leviticus 25:47-49).

The question is, how deep, and in what ways, did the Torah's instructions on the status of slaves influence Shaul's thought here? The answer will take more scholarship and a relevant, in-depth study on the subject of slavery/servitude.[6]

What is relevant to this study is to analyze Shaul's relationship and halakhic instruction to both Onesimus and Philemon, to former slave and former slaveowner. He writes of Onesimus as follows:

> Perhaps the reason he was separated from you for
> a brief period was so that you could have him back
> forever, no longer as a slave but as more than a
> slave, as a dear brother. And that he is, especially to
> me. But how much dearer he must be to you, both
> humanly and in union with the Lord! (Philemon
> 15-16, CJB)

Shaul writes of Onesimus as his "brother" (Gk. *adelphon*); although not Jewish, at least not to our knowledge: "[Onesimus is] no longer . . . a slave but as more than a slave . . . a dear brother. And that he is, especially to me. But how much dearer he must be to you, both humanly and in union with the Lord!" (Philemon 16, CJB). Shaul also calls him "part of my very heart" (Philemon 12, CJB), and "my son" (Gk. *"technou"*; Philemon 10, NIV). Indeed, Shaul could have employed Onesimus as his personal attendant during his house arrest in Rome: "I would dearly have loved to keep him with me, in order for him to serve me in your place while I am in prison because of the Good News" (Philemon 13, CJB). Yet Shaul did not do so.

It is possible that Shaul was advocating for Onesimus freedom when he wrote: "So if you are in fellowship with me, receive him as you would me" (Philemon 17, CJB). Of course, Philemon would receive Shaul as his equal, a free man, and as a precious and respected colleague, teacher, and fellow student of Messiah Yeshua. The phrase "no longer as a slave" in verse 15 also leads us to this conclusion. However, it is possible that Shaul was encouraging Philemon to receive Oneismus back into his household as his servant, but with no punishment and no harm to be inflicted upon him; with any past wrongs fully forgiven. Or was Onesimus being sent back a free man, redeemed by Shaul's promised monetary payment? Shaul may have been affected by principles such as those espoused in Deuteronomy 23:15-16 (16-17 in Hebrew): "Do not extradite a slave to his owner, one who has escaped to you from his owner. He will live with you, in your midst, in the place that he chooses within your gates, for his welfare. You will not mistreat him!" (Deut. 23:16-17, author's translation).

Granted, Onesimus' situation deals with a Gentile slave who had a Gentile owner. Yet, there may have been some residual force from the scripture cited above concerning actions towards escaped slaves that motivated Shaul to advocate for Onesimus to Philemon. Again, I am surmising that the message of the Deuteronomy verses cited above would have been in both Shaul's conscious and subconscious mind as he dealt with this situation.

Whatever the actual relationship between Philemon and Onesimus entailed, Shaul treated Onesimus with respect and dignity. He shared the treasures of the Torah and the identity of the Messiah with Onesimus (who responded positively to this gesture of "keruv,".[7] Shaul then cared enough about Onesimus to advocate for his human value and personal dignity by a letter to Philemon. Accordingly, Shaul as well influenced Onesimus to return to Colossae to rejoin Philemon and help him again, albeit in a presumably different role than before. He states this in his letter to the Colossians:

> Our dear brother Tychicus, who is a faithful worker and fellow-slave in the Lord, will give you all the news about me. I have sent him to you for this very reason — so that you might know how we are, and so that he might encourage you. I have sent him with *Onesimus, the dear and faithful brother, who is one of you*; they will tell you everything that has happened here." (Col. 4:7-9, CJB, italics mine).

In sum, Shaul related to Onesimus as if he was indeed a family member, as the names he uses to describe Onesimus include "brother" (adelphon) and "son" (technon) indicate to us. The use of such language, in particular the term "brother," could be reference to a change of status for Onesimus—from slave to equal. It all depends upon how Shaul was using this term (*'akh* in Hebrew), which is used in the Written Torah to refer to free (i.e. not endentured) Jews (cf. Lev. 25:48). Whether or not Shaul meant it in this specific manner when referring to Onesimus, however, is unclear.

It is here where the aforementioned uncertain identification concerning "which Gamliel was which" looms large. Part of the rationale for my identification of the following Talmudic *aggadot* as attached to Rabban Gamliel the Elder is due to my assumption of his greater wealth in *earlier* 1st century Jerusalem. His grandson's later economic status, *after* the First Roman-Jewish War, may not have been on this same level. As a result of that war, economic collapse occurred in Israel to a great degree. Social and political conditions of post-Temple, late first century Jewish life may have made less likely the ownership of Gentile slaves by rabbinic authorities in Yavneh. And Gamliel II, grandson of Gamliel the Elder, would have been among this latter group of sages. I do pay attention below that Rabbi Joshua is mentioned in the aggadah of Bava Kama 74b, which would seem to argue for the owner of Tabi being Gamliel II. However, the aggadah may be a story that is "intergenerational": that is, giving us a conversation between Gamliel the Elder (d. 50 c.e.) and Rabbi Joshua (d. 131 c.e.) who lived after Gamliel the Elder.

In other words, the students of Rabbi Joshua may be reflecting on the halakha as explained by Gamliel I and kept by Gamliel I's students. The differing opinions are relayed by the use of the name of the rabbi quoted, and thus are tied to his authority and teaching on the given practice. Such intergenerational interplay is common in rabbinic literature. Therefore, in the cited aggadah, is it possible that Joshua ben Hananya's students are commenting upon the halakhic opinion of Rabban Gamliel I, from an earlier era? Close adherence to correct dating and exact historicity is not a given ideal in rabbinic literature. There is no strict adherence to such in ancient literature, as there may be today. My identification remains conjecture, however.

The relevant pericopes that include Tabi are few in the Mishnah, but they nevertheless will constitute our acquaintance with him. Here is one:

> When his household servant Tabi died, he received condolences on his behalf. His students questioned him: 'Our honored rabbi, you taught us that one doesn't receive condolences for servants!' He answered them: 'My servant Tabi wasn't like most servants. He was kosher.' (M. Berakot 2.7, BT, author's translation)

And again:

> Said R. Simeon: It happened that Tabbi, the slave of R. Gamaliel, used to sleep under a bed (during Sukkot). But R. Gamaliel said to the elders: Do you see my slave Tabbi? He is a scholar (*Talmid Hakham*), and knows that slaves are exempt from the duty of Succah. Therefore he sleeps under a bedstead. (Sanhedrin 20b, Soncino translation).

Another aggadah notes:

> It happened that R. Gamaliel [by accident] put out the eye of Tabi his slave. He rejoiced over it very much [as he was eager to have this meritorious slave set free], and when he met R. Joshua he said to him: 'Do you know that Tabi my slave has obtained his freedom?' 'How was that?' said the other. 'Because,' he replied, 'I have [accidentally] put out his eye.' Said R. Joshua to him, 'Your words have no force in law, since there were no witnesses for the slave.' This of course implies that had witnesses at that time been available for the slave, R. Gamaliel would have been under obligation [to set him free]. (Bava Kama 74b, Soncino Edition)

This story informs us that Gamliel wanted his slave to enjoy the rights of a free man. Although a number of points are made by this aggadah, it is clear that it is meant to further the reputation of Gamliel as one who cared about the welfare of his servant, and attempted to apply Torah principles in his behavior towards him.

Tabi was not Jewish, but a descendant of a non-Jewish people, in the category of an '*eved canaani*' (foreign servant). Most often such servants were not agricultural laborers, but domestic servants. This was a common situation in late Second Temple Israel: "One may presume that the majority of slaves in Jewish Palestine in the Second Temple period were of foreign origin, or in terms of the Halakah, 'Canaanite' and not 'Hebrew' slaves".[8] Again, Safrai notes: ". . . when one speaks of slavery in this period, the reference is essentially to Canaanite slaves. . . . one must stress that in effect these foreign slaves became a part of the Jewish people".[9]

It is unclear whether Tabi was personally bought by Gamliel to be his domestic servant (according to Lev. 25:44-45), or came into Gamliel's employ through another way. But we learn of two facts about Gamliel's relationship to Tabi. First, Gamliel had insured Tabi's Torah education. Tabi is called a "talmid hakam" in the Mishnah, meaning he was learned in the Bible, halakah and Jewish tradition. A further inclusion in the Talmud Yerushalmi notes this: Tabi, the servant of R. Gamliel put on tefillin and sages did not protest against him (Yerushalmi Eruvin 10.1, 26a).

We understand that Gamliel honored Tabi by allowing (even teaching him to perform) rituals that were obligatory only for Jews, such as tying tefillin. This boils down to the fact that Gamliel honored his non-Jewish servant (even posthumously).

Gamliel treated Tabi like a member of his flesh-and-blood family. The Sanhedrin sage taught Torah to Tabi, allowed Tabi (at least theoretically) to observe some mitzvot, and finally received condolences for Tabi after his death (akin to sitting *shiva*, if not specifically referring to the actual rite). "At times we hear of the most cordial relations between slaves and their masters . . . these

66

slaves of foreign origin became a part of the Jewish nation and it was customary to circumcise (and thus convert) them".[10] Safrai appears to be accurately describing the relationship between Gamliel and Tabi.

Finally, we must ask, how did the rabbi (Gamliel) affect the student (Shaul) regarding the treatment of slaves? The greatest similarity between rabbi and student is that neither allowed the legal definition of an owner-servant relationship to restrict their connection with the servant with whom they related. Gamliel surprised his students by extending privileges to his servant that were not obligatory, given the social and halakhic situation. Shaul also related to a possible fugitive slave with human respect, and instructed his student to do so, as well. He may have even paid to redeem Onesimus.

However, both of our rabbis conferred basic human dignity upon the servants in question, and did so stemming from their Torah-based perspectives. Tabi was not an 'eved ivri, a fully Jewish servant, subject to all the instructions of the Written Torah (Bible) for Jewish servants. Yet he was treated extremely well by Gamliel, again, as a member of his own family. Neither was Onesimus an 'eved ivri, yet Shaul goes out of his way to help secure Onesimus' dignity and probably legal freedom. Could Gamliel's approach to Gentile slaves have "rubbed off" on Shaul? The probability is certainly there.

Again, I cannot specifically prove that Gamliel taught Shaul anything about the halakha as pertains to slaves. However, it is worthwhile noting that Gamliel and Shaul shared a similar attitude of acting benevolently towards servants in the contexts in which they existed in these two sages' lives.[10] They both upheld the human dignity and worth of the slaves with whom they related.[11]

Conclusion

S haul was educated in the milieu of the 1st century Pharisees. We have seen evidence of such a mindset in his teachings. What we do not find is strict reiteration of teaching from Rabban Gamliel the Elder. Neither does Shaul directly quote a halakha in Gamliel's name, which would be sure evidence of the Rabban's influence on Shaul.

Nevertheless, I have cited a number of Shaul's teachings in which he agrees with the gist, as well as some halakhic stances, of Gamliel. Thus, let me conclude that although textual evidence is not abundant, Gamliel's influence on Shaul was a certainty. This would fit the logic of relationship that existed in that time period: Hillel influenced his students, including his son, the sage Shimon; Shimon influenced his students and his son, the sage Gamliel; and Gamliel influenced his students—all of them.

We do well to remember that the Newer Testament writings were not written for the purpose of purveying the teachings of Rabban Gamliel, nor was any specific section in it written in order to show the relationship of Yeshua's early students to any particular Sanhedrin sage (although we do get a very superficial picture of this through mention of Gamliel the Elder in Acts 5 of Nakdimon (Ben Gurion?, a.k.a. Nicodemus, 1), in John 3, and of Yosef of Ramatayim (a.k.a. Joseph of Aramithea) of John 19:.38 and Mark 15:43).

Last, in spite of the scant textual evidence available, we have seen logical connections and parallels that link Shaul to Gamliel. We can conclude that the influence of the latter upon the former exists for us philosophically and halakhically as we compare their teachings one to the other in the context of the world of first century Pharisaic Judaism.

Appendix:

Gamliel and Shaul on the Messianic Jewish Community

It is valid to ask why did Shaul actively persecute Messianic Jews? Gamliel appeared to be much more accepting of this new Jewish sect. Of course, there is nothing in the ancient Jewish world that obligates any student to be an exact carbon copy of his teacher(s). This alone is reason enough to viably explain the difference between the two teachers. Yet, there may also be more aspects to this difference than meets the eye.

Gamliel did not issue a halakhic ruling stating that Messianic Jews should be persecuted or opposed. At least, none that we know of, and we have no such opinion that is written down. Neither, to our knowledge, did the Great Sanhedrin in Jerusalem issue any such written dictum between the relevant years of 30-70 C.E. In fact, Acts chapter 5 gives us quite the opposite perspective, that Gamliel was all for toleration in this instance. Eisenbaum noted: "Paul's belief in Jesus would not have branded him a heretic.[1] "This is true at this point in time in the first century. Later on, as evidenced in rabbinic literature, it may have been enough to indeed do so.

In modern terms, this is understandable: a group like the Chabad Hasidic movement includes personnel with differing

71

attitudes towards today's Messianic Jewish communities. Some are friendly and tolerant, others, such as activists in the group Yad L'Achim, are staunchly and sometimes militantly opposed. The Chabad movment contains persons of both opinions. Thus it is conceivable that Shaul, a Pharisee of Bet Hillel and student of Gamliel, differed from Gamliel in this matter. It would be unrealistic for us to expect all of Bet Hillel to be of one opinion towards the Messianic Jewish community then. It would also be unrealistic for us to expect all of Chabad's members today to be of one opinion on this matter. My conclusion is that this difference of opinion between teacher and student should not be considered odd or strange. It should not be a bloc to Shaul being considered a close student of Gamliel.

Shaul was not obliged to have the exact same approach as his teacher, since this issue did not have a universal halakhic ruling at that time. This particular situation also may have had a political aspect to it that could not be fully contained in a clearly defined halakhic manner. Lampel noted the ability of students and teachers to disagree on matters:

> Did the disciples ever disagree with their teacher practically, or even academically? The answer is, yes, and this is said without ignoring the dictum (Sanhedrin 10a) . . . 'kol haholeq 'al ravo choleq 'al HaShekinah . . . Whoever differs with rebbi is virtually differing with G-d.' (Lampel, p. 167, transliteration mine)

Although Lampel applies his statement to refer to halakhic disagreements, political ones certainly entered this fray. Such political disagreements occurred between our Torah teachers during the events leading up to the First Roman War, as well as the Second Roman War. It is noteworthy that Lampel cites at least twenty places in rabbinic literature where rabbis and their students disagreed during the period of the Tannaim and Amoraim, punctuating his point with the example of Yehuda ha-Nasi, who in 17 places disagreed with his scholar-father! Yet Lampel emphasizes that normally students *agreed* with their teachers and followed their halakhic understandings. Then, halakhically speaking, Shaul had freedom to understand the situation with Messianic Jews in a way that differed from Rabban Gamliel, which he apparently did.

Additionally, from my lifelong experience as a teacher, I have seen that often students possess a zeal that is above and beyond that of their teacher. At times this leads to action that may not have been authorized nor approved by one's teacher or rabbi. When young, zealous students passionately feel that "they" are the standard by which to measure the correct practice of their faith and traditions, intolerance can be but a small step away. Such young persons can take aggressive actions aimed at others who do not share their opinions or practice, without (or with) their teachers' knowledge and encouragement. In modern Israel, we have had such actions injure people and spread hatred instead of Torah knowledge. It may not have been any different in Gamliel and Shaul's day.

Acts 7:56-57 is a possible expression of such a situation; it is unsure exactly what occurred here, in that there did not appear to be a trial with a decision issued by the Great Sanhedrin in order to convict Stephen of the accused capital crime. Imbedded in this situation is the fact that to a great degree, the Roman overlords had taken away the right of the Great Sanhedrin to even try cases of capital crimes. As Lampel has noted: "At sporadic moments during the Roman rule, the sages were able to convene for discussion and vote" (Lampel, 190). However, the Great Sanhedrin was only partially functioning.

Therefore, the precise nature of gatherings of various sanhedrins (or courts) in Jerusalem, including this one in Acts 7, is not clearly defined for us. This may have been a "kangaroo" court, assembled in conjunction with the High Priest and his allies, which may be what happened previously to Yeshua, as well.

(Given the circumstances, it is highly doubtful that Yeshua was convicted by the Great Sanhedrin.) Given Luke's narrative of the time leading up to Stephen's death, there is indeed some form of a trial that occurred. Yet the narrative lacks what would have been necessary to clearly describe an authentic capital crimes trial by the Great Sanhedrin. This may have been an instance where chaos and prejudice reigned and passions ran high, leading to "quick, in-house justice," and an unauthorized death. It is also uncertain as to how the High Priest would have justified this action legally, unless his political connections to the Roman authorities at that point gave him great leeway in this matter *regarding this new sect in Jerusalem*, whom the Romans may also have perceived as a threat to their Middle Eastern Pax Romana. Thus they may have granted a freer hand to the High Priest, their ally, in attempting to thwart the influence of this movement. Yet this is merely my conjecture, and my private reading of the given text. It is, however, of note that Shaul, in his role as a Messianic Jewish teacher, was also accused of being "seditious" towards the Roman Empire:

> A lawyer named Tertullus . . . presented their case against Sha'ul to the governor. Sha'ul was called, and Tertullus began to make the charges: 'Felix, your Excellency, it is because of you that we enjoy unbroken peace, and it is your foresight that has brought to this nation, so many reforms in so many areas. It is with the utmost gratitude that we receive this. But, in order not to take up too much of your time, I beg your indulgence to give us a brief hearing. We have found this man a pest. He is an agitator among all the Jews throughout the world and a ringleader of the sect of the Natzratim. He even tried to profane the Temple, but we arrested him.' (Acts 24:2-6, CJB)

There were those in the Roman government and in the high priesthood who had the sentiment that this particular sect of Jews posed a political threat to the Pax Romana. Therefore, this false accusation was leveled. Interestingly again, the High Priest is noted as having active involvement in this very accusation: *"The cohen hagadol (High Priest) Hananyah came down with some elders and a lawyer named Tertullus and they presented their case against Sha'ul to the governor"* (Acts 24:1, CJB).

Adding to this perspective, some years prior, Shaul informs us specifically that the Chief Priest authorized his anti-Messianic Jewish actions (cf. Acts 22:5); there is no mention of any involvement in this by any specific Pharisaic authority, including Gamliel. Politically speaking, this is logical, in that the family of the High Priest was quite at odds with Yeshua himself (cf. Lk. 22:3-6, where the high priest's family is specifically mentioned in attempting to harm Yeshua). Thus, for that same enmity to continue to be exhibited by the family of the High Priest towards Yeshua's students is, again, quite understandable.

Chapter Five:

1 Thessalonians 5.23, a Test Case

To better understand Shaul's *sitz im leben,* I am including this short chapter into this essay. In this way, we can understand his strong connection to his first century, Pharisaic, Land of Israel-based Jewish world while he engaged with the Gentile world around him.

Rav Shaul wrote this letter in approximately 50 A.D. (C.E.) as part of his on-going activity of engaging in his responsa with his students in Thessalonika. He corresponded with leading individuals who had become students of Messiah Yeshua, in this city where he had previously visited.

This verse will serve as one single example of possible ways to understand Rav Shaul's writings that consider more of a Jewish perspective. It is admitted that some conjecture is used to help construct the framework by which to view this verse. However, is it believed by the author that such conjecture is based upon solid historical and sociological bases. Our verse in question states: "May the God of *shalom* make you completely holy—may your entire spirit, soul and body be kept blameless for the coming of our Lord Yeshua the Messiah" (CJB).

Another translation states: v. 23: May the God of peace Himself sanctify you completely. May your whole spirit, soul, and body be preserved blameless at the coming of our Lord Yeshua the Messiah (Gruber translation). The Greek text of this verse is as follows:

Αὐτὸς δὲ ὁ θεὸς τῆς εἰρήνης ἁγιάσαι ὑμᾶς ὁλοτελεῖς, καὶ ὁλόκληρον ὑμῶν τὸ πνεῦμα καὶ ἡ ψυχὴ καὶ τὸ σῶμα ἀμέμπτως ἐν τῇ παρουσίᾳ τοῦ κυρίου ἡμῶν Ἰησοῦ Χριστοῦ τηρηθείη.

For some background perspective, Guzik frames this verse in an interesting manner:

> Now may the God of peace Himself sanctify you completely: The idea behind the word "sanctify" is "to set apart"—to make something different and distinct, breaking old associations and forming a new association. For example, a dress is a dress; but a wedding dress is *sanctified*—set apart for a special, glorious purpose. God wants us to be *set apart* to Him. (taken from http://www.studylight.org/com/guz/view.cgi?book=1th&chapter=005).

Guzik's comment puts this verse into a valid perspective. Guzik is telling us that Shaul is talking about "holiness" in our given verse. The Greek word used in this verse, *hagiasai,* reflects a cognate to the Hebrew, to the word used in the Torah, *kadosh.* The UBS Hebrew version of the Newer Testament (publ. 1976) uses the word *yekadesh* in translating Shaul's word *hagiasai,* confirming this connection in the minds of modern Israeli translators. The earlier published (1970) UBS translation uses the same *yekadesh,* as well, for *hagiasai.*

In Jewish thought of both Shaul's time down until today, "holy" means to be separated in order to serve the One God. Thus, people can be holy, that is, they can dedicate and separate their lives to the end of loving and serving God. Objects and time can be "holy" in Jewish thought, as well.

Therefore, the Sabbath (the 7th day, presented in its given *time-related* frame) is separated from the other days of the week, rendering it "holy." A Torah scroll is separated from other writings, books or literature, due to its purpose and end. Thus, it is "holy," with a developed set of customs regarding how to handle it, when to read it publicly, and how to care for it, all of which emphasize its separateness, its specialness, and thus its "holiness." The reader is encouraged to study the concept of "kadosh" (holy) or "kedushah"(holiness) in Jewish thought for more insight into this particular subject matter.

In agreement with Guzik, our text is speaking about a person being "holy"; that is, one who has given his life (or dedicated it) to God, in order to carry out God's purposes. In 1st century Jewish thought, this meant that individuals would carry out the message and instructions of the Written Torah in their given community. This concept has remained a stable and consistent one throughout Jewish history. And thus, the CJB translation of this verse, in stating: ". . . make you completely holy," contains, I believe, the proper emphasis on the main issue being addressed by the rabbi—that of *kedushah*, קדושה, holiness; that is, the dedicating of one's life to carrying out the teachings of the Written Torah, as interpreted by one's community and rabbi(s).

Now, let us briefly analyze the Jewish context of our text. "The shema", found in Deuteronomy 6.4-6, states:

> Hear, O Israel: The Lord is our God; the Lord is one. And you shall love the Lord, your God, with all your heart and with all your soul and with all your means. And these words, which I command you this day, shall be upon your heart. (Deut. 6:4-6, Chabad translation)

Another rendition states:

> Sh'ma, Yisra'el! ADONAI Eloheinu, ADONAI
> echad [Hear, Isra'el! ADONAI our God, ADONAI
> is one]; and you are to love ADONAI your God with
> all your heart, all your being and all your resources.
> These words, which I am ordering you today, are to
> be on your heart. (CJB)

The Masoretic Hebrew text states:

שמע יצראל יהוה אלהינו יהוה אתד
ואהבת את יהוה אלהיך בכל לבבך ובכל נפשך ובכל מאדך
והיו הדברים האלה אשר אנכי מצוך היום על
לבבך

These verses describe the way in which "holiness" was conceived
of in biblical thought. One's "lev," לב (mind), "nefesh," נפש (life),
and "me'od," מאוד (physical resources, energy and efforts) are
the three areas included in this concept within these verses. To
paraphrase the verses, then: "Pay attention and act upon this:
Adonay is our God, Adonay is One. Therefore, love Adonay your
God with all of your thoughts, with all of your life and with all of
your resources. So then these words that I command you today will
be in your minds!" This is a conceptual paraphrase that I believe
captures the thrust of these three verses. These verses would have
been the foundational, conceptual, and textual bases for Rav Shaul
when he taught his students about dedicating their lives to serving
the One God of Israel. In other words, Deuteronomy 6:4-6 would
have been what Shaul had in mind when he wrote 1 Thessalonians
5:23, in that the subject matter of these two sets of verses is similar.

The Koine text itself purveys Jewish concepts, not a Hellenist
mindset. Thus, the use of the Greek works "pneuma," "psuche,"
and "soma," instead of taking on its possible pagan, Hellenist
definitions, must be seen in their Torah-based, biblical, and Jewish

backgrounds. When we do so, we can emerge with a much better idea of just what the rabbi was telling his students in Thessalonica 5:23 should be seen in the light in which Gruber frames the Koine writings of Rav Shaul:

> The concepts and definitions remained Hebrew even though the translated appearance of the language was Greek. . . . The Scriptures use Greek words in ways that the Greeks did not, and also use words which the Greeks did not know. (Gruber, 78-79, 82-83)

In this verse, the rabbi was not encouraging the dichotomy of thought that existed in the Hellenist world, where a person is sliced into different "parts" (e.g. a body, a soul, and a spirit), each which operated independent of, and sometimes in opposition to, the others. Such a definition of a person is not a Torah nor biblically based one, which is better reflected by this description:

> The biblical conception . . . views the soul as part of the psychophysical unity of man, who, by his very nature, is composed of a body and a soul. As such, the Bible is dominated by a monistic view . . . for it sees in man only his tangible body and views the soul simply as that element that imparts to the body its vitality. The soul is, indeed, considered the site of the emotions, but not of a spiritual life separate from that of the body, or of a mental or emotional life in conflict with that of the body, it is, rather, the seat of all of man's feelings and desires, physical as well as spiritual. Such a conception views the entire entity of man as a "living soul," or, to put it in our terms, a psychophysical organism created in the image of God. (taken from: http://www.myjewishlearning.com/beliefs/Theology/

Afterlife_and_Messiah/Life_After_Death/
Immortality/Spirituality_and_the_Soul)

This author agrees with the analysis stating:

> Attempts at interpreting Paul exclusively or
> primarily against a Hellenistic background are
> fundamentally misguided and will produce
> distortion. With perhaps a few exceptions, the
> influence of Hellenism on Paul's theology is minor,
> usually ad hoc formulations resulting from disputes
> with opponents who had introduced Hellenistic
> views into the church or theological formulations
> assumed by Paul from the early church. (http://
> www.abu.nb.ca/courses/pauline/Introd.htm)

With the above in mind, the connecting of 1 Thessalonians 5:23
to its conceptual root, found in Deuteronomy 6, allows us to
understand the concept of "holiness" as Shaul did. In turn, we
can then understand what he was saying. When seen in its Jewish
framework, this verse is consistent with what any 1st century rabbi
would have taught on "being holy," and these words in Koine find
their conceptual parallels in the very words of the Written Torah.
Such an understanding provides a consistent reading of Shaul's
writings with that of the Jewish and rabbinic world of which he
was a part. It was *this* world that educated and raised him; it was
this world's truths, found in the words of the Written Torah, that
provided Shaul with his teaching material to his students. Indeed,
he fondly recalls this very world, of which he always considered
himself a part:

> . . . the people of Isra'el! They were made God's
> children, the *Sh'khinah* (God's presence) has been
> with them, the covenants are theirs, likewise the
> giving of the *Torah*, the Temple service and the

> promises; the Patriarchs are theirs; and from them,
> as far as his physical descent is concerned, came
> the Messiah, who is over all. Praised be *ADONAI*
> forever! *Amen.* (Rom. 9:4-5, CJB)

When they had gathered, he said to them: "Brothers, *although I have done nothing against either our people or the traditions of our fathers*, I was made a prisoner in Yerushalayim and handed over to the Romans (Acts 28:17, CJB, italics mine, for emphasis).

Being that the rabbi continued to identify himself as a strictly Torah observant Jew in approximately 60 C.E., when the event in Rome described above occurred, it is only logical that his belief systems would have continued to be those of his upbringing, as well. Clearly from the above verses, we understand that the concepts of covenant, of Israel's election, of the value of the Torah, of the value of Messiah, and of the validity of Pharisaic tradition, had not ever been lost upon Shaul.

Therefore, the proposed understanding of 1 Thessalonians 5:23 fits well into a 1st century Jewish framework. Any understanding that would fashion Shaul's statement into a "new" theology, or into a Hellenist framework, would have departed from what he stated at the end of his life (cf. Acts 28:17). Thus, any such understanding would be highly illogical.

Glossary

Aggadah: A story used to illustrate a principle, or inform us of a sage and his teachings or behavior.

Agunah: A woman who legally cannot change her marriage status from married to single, due to a number of halakhic reasons.

Amoraim: The sages quoted in the Gemara, commenting upon the Mishna's halakhic rulings.

Avodah: This word can mean "worship," "physical work," or "idolatry," depending upon the context of its usage.

Avot d'Rabbi Natan: A midrashic and aggadic text from the Gaonic time period.

Avot: Or more fully, "Pirke Avot," is a tractate of the Mishnah.

Bat Kol or Bath Kol: A "Heavenly voice" that is attested to in Talmudic aggadot.

Berit milah: A circumcision or a circumcision ceremony.

Bet Hillel: One of the Pharisaic branches in the first century that looked to the halakhic decisions of Hillel as its foundation.

Bet Midrash: a study center for adults, where traditional texts are taught and studied.

Darkey No'am: An interpretational attitude leading to flexible halakhic rulings that enable the Torah to be kept by the people.

'Eved canaani: Hebrew for the category of foreign servants.

Gemara: The newer portion of the Talmud, commenting upon the Mishnah.

Go'el: Hebrew for the person who monetarily redeemed a relative out of indentured servitude (see Leviticus 25:47-50).

Goy: This is the Hebrew word for "nation"; in vernacular language it refers to non-Jews.

Halakha: A legal ruling in the Jewish community concerning the application of the Torah.

Hamle'kah: Physical work, a profession; sometimes 'craft,' handiwork.

HaShem: A Hebrew name for God, literally, "the Name."

Hora'at ha'sha'ah: Literally, 'Instruction of the hour'; it is an halakhic decision given to deal with a given situation, possibly an emergency, with the particular and possibly rarer circumstances of the given case in mind.

Mahloket (pl. Mahlokot): An halakhic disputation(s) or debate with the end to arrive at the proper halakhic decisions.

Mekhilta: A commentary on the Book of Exodus. According to our tradition, it was written by R. Ishmael, the renowned 2nd century sage and scholar.

Minyan: A group of 10 or more Jewish males, aged 13 or above, who pray together at any given time. It is, among most of the orthodox world, the ideal to pray in a minyan.

Mishnah: The older portion of the Talmud, edited under the initiative of Rabbi Yehudah ha-Nasi.

Mitzvah: (plural: mitzvot) An instruction found in the Bible and/or connected instructions later developed by rabbinic authorities.

Nasi: The role of the chief officer of the Sanhedrin. Hillel and Gamliel the Elder both filled this role, as did Yehudah ha-Nasi (later).

Oleh: An immigrant to Israel, or a pilgrim to Jerusalem for one of the mo'edim (Leviticus 23 times or holy days).

Parush: A Pharisee.

Pax Romana: Latin for the "Roman Peace," referring to the Empire as a non-contested political entity under the control of the Roman nobility, without rebellion from the different ethnic groups comprising the Empire.

Perutah: A coin that was the least in worth and value, used as a standard for Bet Hillel's marriage contracting.

Peshat: Usually, the literal meaning of a verse of Torah.

Pikuah Nefesh: The concept of suspending certain halakhic practices to insure the saving of a life. It is "the obligation to save a life in jeopardy" (Jewish Virtual Library). An example: the early Hasmoneans (approx.165 B.C.E.) decided they would fight on the Sabbath, in order to defend the lives of their communities, which had been attacked by Seleucid military forces on previous Sabbaths.

Pilpul: Literally, "peppering"; a passionate arguing of halakhic viewpoints done to find the best interpretation and application for the given question.

Rabban: An honorific title given to leading sages of a generation, and to the Nasi in particular. It was first given, as far as we know, to Gamliel the Elder.

Rebbe: This is often a Hasidic term used for a "rabbi."

Responsa: Most often, a technical term referring to rabbis' communications on given questions from Jewish communities. In our context, it is used loosely as a non-technical term, to describe the *type* of "question and answer" communication that Shaul had with the communities where he served as rabbi.

Shiva: The custom of sitting in mourning for 7 days after one's parent, sibling, or child has died. Neighbors, wider family and friends come to comfort the given mourner.

Sicarii: A small political group in 1st century Israel that believed in rising up against the Roman occupation to secure freedom. They were known for their use of 'sicae,' a particular weapon that they carried with them.

Talmid Hakham: The leading, senior student of a yeshiva or rabbi.

Tannaim: The sages who are quoted in the Mishnah.

Tefillin: cf. Numbers 15:37; these are the phylacteries that are tied around the arm and that sit on the forehead while praying in the morning.

The Shema: This is Deuteronomy 6:4-6, recited at various times by Jewish individuals during prayers and rituals.

Torah: Usually the first Five Books of Moses, but often refers to any instruction that is given by a teacher who is in the rabbinic chain of transmission.

Zealots: A 1st century group in Israel that lobbied hard for armed uprising against the Roman occupation.

Partial Bibliography

Bonchek, Avigdor. *Studying the Torah*. Aronson, Inc.: Northvale, N.J, 1996.

Chilton, B. and Neusner, J. "Paul and Gamliel". *Bulletin for Biblical Research* 14.1 (2004) 1-43.

Eisenbaum, Pamela. *Paul was not a Christian*. Harper One: N.Y., N.Y, 2009.

Fischer, John. "A Jewish View of Galatians". Unpublished essay, no date given.

Flusser, David. *Jesus*. Magnes Press: Jerusalem, Israel, 1998.

Friedman, David. *They Loved the Torah*. Lederer Publications: Baltimore, MD, 2001.

Friedman, David and Friedman, B.D. *James the Just: Yaakov Hatzaddik Presents Applications of Torah*. Lederer Publications: Baltimore, MD, 2012.

Grant, Michael. *The Jews in the Roman World*. Barnes and Noble: N.Y., N.Y., 1973.

Gruber, D. *The Messianic Writings*. Hanover, N.H.: Elijah Publishing. 2011.

Hegg, Tim. *Paul the Letter Writer*. First Fruits of Zion: Marshfield, MO, 2002.

Lampel, Zvi. *The Dynamics of Dispute*. Judaica Press: Brooklyn, N.Y., 1992.

Lerner, P. Private conversation, Jerusalem, Israel, 7/11/2013.

Mason, Steve. *Flavius Josephus on the Pharisees.* Brill Publications: Leiden, The Netherlands, 1991.

Nanos, Mark. *The Irony of Galatians.* Fortress Press: Minneapolis, MN, 2002.

Notley, S. and Safrai, Z. *Parables of the Sages.* Carta: Jerusalem, Israel, 2011.

Pritz, R. *Nazarene Jewish Christianity.* Magnes Press: Jerusalem, Israel, 1992.

Raz, Simcha. *A Tsaddik in Our Time.* Feldheim Publishers: N.Y., N,Y., 1976.

Scherman, Nosson, translator and commentator. *The Complete Art Scroll Siddur.* Mesorah Publications: Brooklyn, N.Y., 1984.

Shannon, Dror. *Study on Galatians, CAY Study Haverah.* Unpublished study, no date given.

Shulam, J. and LeCornu, H. *The Jewish Roots of Galatians.* Netivyah: Jerusalem, Israel, no date given.

Sicker, Martin. The Moral Maxims of the Sages of Israel: Pirkei Avot. IUniverse: Bloomington, IND., 2004.

Skarsaune, O. and Hvalvik, R., editors. *Jewish Believers in Jesus.* Hendrickson Publishers: Peabody, MA., 2007.

Stern, David, translator. *Complete Jewish Bible.* JNT Publications: Clarksville, MD.,1988.

Stern, M. and Safrai, S. *The Jewish People in the First Century, vols. I and II.* Brill Publications: Leiden, The Netherlands, 1974.

Tomson, Peter. *Paul and the Jewish Law.* VanGorcum Press: Assen, The Netherlands, 1990.

United Bible Societies, publisher. *Sifray ha-berit ha-hadasha.* Yanetz, Ltd.: Jerusalem, Israel, 1976.

Yeroushalmi, David. "The Judeo-Persian Poet 'Emrani and His Book of Treasure", EJ Brill Publications: Leiden, The Netherlands, 1995.

Electronic

Abramowitz, Henry. *Rabban Gamliel and Rabbi Yehoshua in the Analytic Training Institute: A Talmudic Text* (Berachot 27b-28a) and the Group Life of Analysts. Found at: http://www.junginstitute.org/pdf_files/JungV6N2p21-40.pdf

Aghion, Philippe, and Jean Tirole. 1997. "Formal and real authority in organizations." Journal of Political Economy 105(1): 1-29. Accessed from: http://nrs.harvard.edu/urn-3:HUL.InstRepos:4554125

http://www.biblegateway.com/resources/commentaries/IVP-NT/Phlm/Pauls-Greetings

http://www.come-and-hear.com/babakamma/babakamma_74.html

http://www.jewishvirtuallibrary.org/jsource/Talmud/sukkah2.html

http://www.myjewishlearning.com/beliefs/Theology/Afterlife_and_Messiah/Life_After_Death/Immortality/Spirituality_and_the_Soul

http://www.razzberrypress.com/jewish_phrases_and_idioms.html

http://www.readthespirit.com/explore/2009/9/1/508-interview-with-the-scholar-who-writes-paul-was-not-a-chr.html

http://www.sacred-texts.com/jud/t01/t0110.htm

http://www.shechem.org/torah/avot.html

http://www.shemayisrael.com/parsha/kahn/archives/korach65.htm

Jacobs, Louis. 'Rabban Gamliel', http://www.myjewishlearning.com/texts/Rabbinics/Talmud/Mishnah/Mishnah_and_its_Times/Rabban_Gamaliel.shtml

http://www.studylight.org/com/guz/

http://www.oceansidejc.org/roshhash/MishRoshH_02.htm

http://www.come-and-hear.com/sanhedrin/sanhedrin_11.html#PARTb

http://www.laparola.net/greco/louwnida.php.

http://www.thefoundationstone.org/en/podcasts/119-toolsanger/3609-14.html

http://vbm-torah.org/archive/avot/19avot.htm

http://halakah.com/pdf/moed/Eiruvin.pdf

http://www.come-and-hear.com/sanhedrin/sanhedrin_88.html#PARTb

http://www.chabad.org/library/article_cdo/aid/953564/jewish/Rabbi-Yochanans-Request.htm)

http://www.rabbiirons.org/product_info.php?products_id=324

Yadin, Azzan. "Rabban Gamliel, Aphrodite's Bath, and the Question of pagan Monotheism",http://jqr.pennpress.org/PennPress/journals/jqr/JQR200602001.pdf

Disclaimer: Author assumes no responsibility for the upkeep of the websites that are quoted.

End Notes

Chapter One

1. Chilton and Neusner, p.2.

2. On a recent visit to Corinth, my Greek hosts explained to me the reputation that Corinth had in the mid-first century world: a port city full of indulgence, vice, and luxury. In the 1st century, it was a prosperous metropolis with many Italian inhabitants. Shaul's letters reflect some of the societal difficulties that he encountered there, granted that these may have existed in any major ancient metropolis.

2. As found in the Jewish Encyclopedia, quoted from: http://www.geni. com/people/Rabban-Gamliel-I-Hazaken-רבן-גמליאל-הזקן-נשיא- הסנהדרין/6000000001288397755

3. Taken from: http://jqr.pennpress.org/PennPress/journals/jqr/ JQR200602001.pdf

4. Ibid.

5. As quoted in http://www.jewishvirtuallibrary.org/jsource/Talmud/ shabbat16.html

6. As quoted in http://www.jewishvirtuallibrary.org/jsource/Talmud/ rh2.html

7. Ibid.

8. Ibid.

9. As quoted in http://www.jewishvirtuallibrary.org/jsource/Talmud/ shabbat16.htm

10. As a side note, we may have that very image relayed to us in Luke chapter 10, where it is recorded that: "She [Martha] had a sister called Miryam who also sat at the Lord's feet and heard what he had to say" (Lk. 10:39, CJB). Here again, προς τους ποδας pros tous podas, "in front of the feet," is the spatial language used in the verse. Miryam is sitting "at the feet" of her rabbi, indicating that she literally sat in front of his feet, or that she was in a listening and learning mode as a student (or very possibly both). We may understand that Shaul was in a listening and learning mode towards Rabban Gamliel as one of his students, by his description of his proximal position to the sage as relayed in Acts 22:3.

11. Louw and Nida, entry 9.32.

12. Porcius Festus had been just appointed as Procurator, and died shortly thereafter, about the time that Shaul died (approx. 62 a.d.).

Chapter Two

1. Although it is impossible to pinpoint the years in this case, one can estimate that Nitai and his Sanhedrin colleague, Yehoshua, lived about 100 years prior to Shaul's career. I call Nitai "pro-Pharisaic" instead of "Pharsaic," only because it is difficult to know when to apply the term "Pharisee" in generations prior to Hillel and Shammai. Yet I consider Nitai and Shaul to have been, in history, in the same general grouping of Torah sages.

2. On a recent visit to Corinth, my Greek hosts explained to me the reputation that Corinth had in the mid-first century world: a port city full of indulgence, vice, and luxury. In the 1st century, it was a prosperous metropolis with many Italian inhabitants. Shaul's letters reflect some of the societal difficulties that he encountered there, granted that these may have existed in any major ancient metropolis.

3. According to Pirke Avot, five generations of teachers would have separated them in time (Nitai and Yehoshua [generation 1], Yehudah and Shimon [generation 2, which we know was during the lifetime of King Alexander Yannai], Shemaiah and Avtalyon [generation 3], Hillel and Shammai [generation 4], Shimon ben Hillel [generation 5], and then Rabban Gamliel [generation 6].

4. Tosefta Qiddushin 1.11, as quoted in Notley and Safrai, p. 83.

5. Rabbi Levin (d. 1969) immigrated to Mandated Palestine, and became the altruistic rabbi of the Jewish Underground prisoners. His legacy can be seen at the Underground Prisoners' Museum today in Jerusalem.

6. Yet it is impossible to separate between studying Torah texts and living one's life in accordance with what is written in these very texts. Thus, in encouraging his students to be bold, it is implied that they must carry Torah knowledge over into their practice (their orthopraxy). Timothy, as a Jewish teacher of the Torah, would of necessary had to have been well-schooled in the scriptures. In fact, Shaul remarked to him: ". . . from childhood you have known the Holy Scriptures, which can give you the wisdom that leads to deliverance through trusting in Yeshua the Messiah (2 Tim. 3:15, CJB), and was now being encouraged by Shaul, his rabbi, to be bold in his orthopraxy, that is, in his application of the Torah in his role as a leader.

7. Flusser, p. 106.

Chapter 3

1. *Pikuah nefesh* refers to the halakhic principle that someone in physical danger, particularly in a life or death situation, may abandon custom or extant interpretation in order to avoid possible death or severe pain. It is "the obligation to save a life in jeopardy" (Jewish Virtual Library).

2. As quoted in Notley and Safrai, p. 29.

Chapter 4

1. "Servant" or "slave" is a difficult category to define cross-culturally at this time in the ancient world. *Doulon*, the Greek word used, may be synonymous with the Hebrew word *'eved.* The differences between the terms "servant" and "slave" in the ancient Roman Empire cannot be researched in this essay. However, Israel was part of the Roman Empire, and thus Roman law and Jewish Torah (mitzvot) were both in vogue in terms of defining a servant's relationship to his owner, with other social and political factors determining the details and practice.

2. Taken from: http://www.unrv.com/culture/roman-slavery.php

3. Ibid.

4. Ibid.

5. http://saints.sqpn.com/saint-onesimus/

6. I acknowledge the thought of Israeli scholar P. Lerner, who first brought up this subject matter with some of its possibilities to me.

7. "Keruv" is Hebrew for an effort to draw someone close to G-d. Here Shaul does this with a non-Jew, which he considered to be a role of the people of Israel (that is, the Jewish people) among the nations.

8. Safrai and Stern, p. 629. Prof. Safrai, of blessed memory, emphasized that there are no examples of Jewish slaves in Jewish families in late Second Temple times. See p. 629, *The Jewish People in the First Century.*

9. Ibid., p. 630.

10. Interestingly, regarding the identification of Rabban Gamliel, Gittin 56a records that Rabbi Joshua was one of the students of Rabban Yohanan, and he fled the destruction of Jerusalem in 70 C.E. safely, along with his rabbi. One stream of thought states that both Rabbi Gamliel the Elder and his grandson Gamliel II had slaves named Tabi! Perhaps this reflects the fact that clear historical evidence to identify which "Gamliel was Gamliel" has been unsure throughout the past 2,000 years.

11. If, however, as some imply, Tabi was converted and became at some point fully and halakhhically Jewish, then Gamliel would have been obliged to treat Tabi according to all the mitzvot concerning a fellow Jew. Evidence is lacking to prove this particular slant to the situation, however. In fact, the mishna addressing Tabi's death and Gamliel's ensuing halakhic behavior would seem to argue for the opposite case: that Tabi never fully reached the legal status of a Jewish male.

Conclusion

1. Nakdimon ben Gurion was a first century Sanhedrin sage, and could be the Nicodemus of John chapter 3. Ben Gurion was noted as one of the richest and most generous persons in Jerusalem prior to the First Roman War. See Gittim 56a and Ketuvim 66b for possible reference to him,

Appendix

1. Eisenbaum, p. 8.

2. Chabad is the name for the Lubavitcher Hasidic sect, today headquartered in New York City, with many offices around the world. The movement has been very influential, especially among young adults in the Diaspora.

OTHER RELATED RESOURCES

Available at Messianic Jewish Resources Int'l. • www.messianicjewish.net
1-800-410-7367
(Check our website for current discounts and promotions)

First Time in History!

General Editor: Rabbi Barry Rubin
Theological Editor: Dr. John Fischer

The Complete Jewish Study Bible

Insights for Jews and Christians
—Dr. David H. Stern

< Hardcover Edition

A One-of-a-Kind Study Bible that illuminates the Jewish background and context of God's word so it is more fully understandable. Uses the updated *Complete Jewish Bible* text by David H. Stern, including notes from the *Jewish New Testament Commentary* and contributions from Scholars listed below. 1990 pages.

Hardback	978-1619708679	$49.95
Flexisoft	978-1619708693	$79.95
Leather	978-1619708709	$139.95

Leather Edition w/color gift box   Flexisoft Edition w/color sleeve

CONTRIBUTORS & SCHOLARS

Rabbi Dr. Glenn Blank	Forbes	Rabbi Barney Kasdan	Rosenberg
Dr. Michael Brown	Rabbi Dr. David	Dr. Craig S. Keener	Rabbi Isaac Roussel
Rabbi Steven Bernstein	Friedman	Rabbi Elliot Klayman	Dr. Michael Rydelnik
Rabbi Joshua	Dr. Arnold	Jordan Gayle Levy	Dr. Jeffrey Seif
Brumbach	Fruchtenbaum	Dr. Ronald Moseley	Rabbi Tzahi Shapira
Rabbi Ron Corbett	Dr. John Garr	Rabbi Dr. Rich Nichol	Dr. David H. Stern
Pastor Ralph Finley	Pastor David Harris	Rabbi Mark J. Rantz	Dr. Bruce Stokes
Rabbi Dr. John Fischer	Benjamin Juster	Rabbi Russ Resnik	Dr. Tom Tribelhorn
Dr. Patrice Fischer	Rabbi Dr. Daniel Juster	Dr. Richard Robinson	Dr. Forrest Weiland
Rebbitzen Malkah	Dr. Walter C. Kaiser	Rabbi Dr. Jacob	Dr. Marvin Wilson

QUOTES BY JEWISH SCHOLARS & SAGES

Dr. Daniel Boyarin
Dr. Amy-Jill Levine
Rabbi Jonathan Sacks
Rabbi Gamaliel
Rabbi Hillel
Rabbi Shammai
Rabbi Akiva
Maimonides
and many more

Complete Jewish Bible: *An English Version*

—Dr. David H. Stern (Available March 2017)

Now, the most widely used Messianic Jewish Bible around the world, has updated text with introductions added to each book, written from a biblically Jewish perspective. The CJB is a unified Jewish book, a version for Jews and non-Jews alike; to connect Jews with the Jewishness of the Messiah, and non-Jews with their Jewish roots. Names and terms are returned to their original Hebrew and presented in easy-to-understand transliterations, enabling the reader to say them the way *Yeshua* (Jesus) did! 1728 pages.

Paperback	978-1936716845	$29.95
Hardcover	978-1936716852	$34.95
Flexisoft Cover	978-1936716869	$49.95

Jewish New Testament
—Dr. David H. Stern

The New Testament is a Jewish book, written by Jews, initially for Jews. Its central figure was a Jew. His followers were all Jews; yet no other version really communicates its original, essential Jewishness. Uses neutral terms and Hebrew names. Highlights Jewish references and corrects mistranslations. Freshly translated into English from Greek, this is a must read to learn about first-century faith. 436 pages

Hardback	978-9653590069	**JB02**	$19.99
Paperback	978-9653590038	**JB01**	$14.99
Spanish	978-1936716272	**JB17**	$24.99

Also available in French, German, Polish, Portuguese and Russian.

Jewish New Testament Commentary
—Dr. David H. Stern

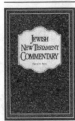

This companion to the *Jewish New Testament* enhances Bible study. Passages and expressions are explained in their original cultural context. 15 years of research. 960 pages.

Hardback	978-9653590083	**JB06**	$34.99
Paperback	978-9653590113	**JB10**	$29.99

A Life of Favor
A Family Therapist Examines the Story of Joseph and His Brothers
—Rabbi Russell Resnik, MA, LPCC

Favor is an inherent part of God's reality as Father, and properly understood, is a source of blessing to those who want to know him. The story of Jacob's sons points to a life of favor that can make a difference in our lives today. Excellent insight—judgments in exegesis are matched by skillful use of counseling principles and creative applications to contemporary situations in life and in the family. —Walter C. Kaiser, Jr. President Emeritus, Gordon-Conwell Theological Seminary, Hamilton, Mass. 212 Pages

Paperback	978-1936716913	$19.99

Will the Nazi Eagle Rise Again?
What the Church Needs to Know about BDS and Other Forces of Anti-Semitism
–David Friedman, Ph.D.

This is the right book at the right time. exposing the roots of Anti-Semitism being resurrected in our days, especially in our Christian Church.
—Dr. Hans-Jörg Kagi, Teacher, Theologian, Basle, Switzerland

Timely and important response to the dangerous hatred of the State of Israel that is growing in society and in the Church.
—Michael Rydelnik, Prof. of Jewish Studies, Moody Bible Inst., Chicago, Ill.

Israel is not an apartheid state and bears absolutely no resemblance to the institutionalized racial oppression that I lived under in South Africa. I am deeply offended by this comparison.
—Luba Mayekiso, Africa for Israel Christian Coalition, Republic of South Africa

Paperback (278 Pages)	978-1936716876	$19.99

The Day Jesus Did Tikkun Olam
—Richard A. Robinson, Ph.D.

Easy-to-read, yet scholarly, explores ancient Jewish and Christian scriptures, relevant stories and biblical parallels, to explain the most significant Jewish value—*tikkun olam*—making this world a better place. This is a tenet of both religions, central to the person of Jesus himself.
—Murray Tilles, Director, Light of Messiah Ministries; M.Div.

A wealth of scholarship and contemporary relevance with great insight into Jewish ethics and the teachings of Jesus.
—Dr. Richard Harvey, Senior Researcher, Jews for Jesus

146 pages	978-1-936716-98-2	$ 18.99

Zipporah's Farm
—Written by Ani Perez, Illustrated by Deborah Wilson

I believe animals are a gift that God has given to us for our pleasure. They should be loved and protected. They are innocent and never should be killed for sport. I welcome you to my farm, where there is an abundance of love, peace and joy. It is a place where anyone at any age can escape into fantasy and forget about the world's troubles, even if only for a little while. Welcome to Zipporah's Farm.
Large 8.5 x 11 inches, 60 pages, with full color illustrations.

Hardcover	978-1-936716-97-5	$24.99
Paperback	978-1-936716-96-8	$19.99

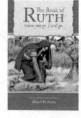

The Book of Ruth

This delightful version of *The Book of Ruth* includes the full text from the *Complete Jewish Bible* on the left page of the two-page spread. On the right are artful illustrations with brief story summaries that can be read to young children. Can be read any time during the year, but especially on *Shavuot* (Pentecost), the anniversary of the giving of the Torah on Mount Sinai and when the Holy Spirit was poured out on Yeshua's disciples (Acts 2). *The Book of Ruth* points to Yeshua as the ultimate Kinsman Redeemer.
6 x 9 inches, 26 pages with full color illustrations.

978-1-936716-94-4	$ 9.99

The Book of Esther

This delightful version of *The Book of Esther* includes the full text from the *Complete Jewish Bible* on the left page of the two-page spread. On the right are artful illustrations with brief story summaries that can be read to young children. Can be read any time during the year, but especially during *Purim*, the festival that celebrates how Queen Esther risked her life and became a vessel for the deliverance of her people Israel. Though God is not mentioned, Mordecai and Esther humbled themselves before God by fasting and praying, which showed dependence upon him. God answered and delivered his people while bringing the proud Haman to justice.
6 x 9 inches, 34 pages with full color illustrations.

978-1-936716-95-1	$ 9.99

Jewish Giftedness & World Redemption
The Calling of Israel
—Jim Melnick

All things are mortal but the Jew; all other forces pass, but he remains. What is the secret of his immortality?
—Mark Twain, Concerning the Jews, *Harper's Magazine*, September, 1899.

The most comprehensive research of the unique achievements of the Jewish people. The author comes up with the only reason that makes sense of this mystery.
—Daniel C. Juster, Th.D., Restoration from Zion of Tikkun International
        Paperback (280 Pages)   978-1-936716-88-3 $24.99

Messianic Judaism *A Modern Movement With an Ancient Past*
—David H. Stern

An updated discussion of the history, ideology, theology and program for Messianic Judaism. A challenge to both Jews and non-Jews who honor Yeshua to catch the vision of Messianic Judaism. 312 pages
                    978-1880226339   **LB62** $17.99

Restoring the Jewishness of the Gospel
A Message for Christians
—David H. Stern

Introduces Christians to the Jewish roots of their faith, challenges some conventional ideas, and raises some neglected questions: How are both the Jews and "the Church" God's people? Is the Law of Moses in force today? Filled with insight! Endorsed by Dr. Darrell L. Bock. 110 pages
        English   978-1880226667   **LB70** $9.99
        Spanish   978-9653590175   **JB14** $9.99

The Return of the Kosher Pig *The Divine Messiah in Jewish Thought*
—Rabbi Tzahi Shapira

The subject of Messiah fills many pages of rabbinic writings. Hidden in those pages is a little known concept that the Messiah has the same authority given to God. Based on the Scriptures and traditional rabbinic writings, this book shows the deity of Yeshua from a new perspective. You will see that the rabbis of old expected the Messiah to be divine. Softcover, 352 pages.
"One of the most interesting and learned tomes I have ever read. Contained within its pages is much with which I agree, some with which I disagree, and much about which I never thought. Rabbi Shapria's remarkable book cannot be ignored."
—Dr. Paige Patterson, President, Southwest Baptist Theological Seminary
                    978-1936716456   **LB81** $ 39.99

Proverbial Wisdom & Common Sense

A Messianic Commentary

—Derek Leman

A Messianic Jewish Approach to Today's Issues from the Proverbs
A devotional style commentary, divided into chapters suitable for daily
reading. An encyclopedia of practical advice on topics relevant to everyone.
248 pages

Paperback 978-1880226780 **LB98** $19.99

Matthew Presents Yeshua, King Messiah *A Messianic Commentary*

—Rabbi Barney Kasdan

Few commentators are able to truly present Yeshua in his Jewish context.
Most don't understand his background, his family, even his religion, and
consequently really don't understand who he truly is. This commentator is
well versed with first-century Jewish practices and thought, as well as the
historical and cultural setting of the day, and the 'traditions of the Elders'
that Yeshua so often spoke about. Get to know Yeshua, the King, through
the writing of another rabbi, Barney Kasdan. 448 pages

978-1936716265 **LB76** $29.99

Rabbi Paul Enlightens the Ephesians on Walking with Messiah Yeshua

A Messianic Commentary

—Rabbi Barney Kasdan

The Ephesian were a diverse group of Jews and Gentiles, united together in
Messiah. They definitely had an impact on the first century world in which
they lived. But the Rabbi was not just writing to that local group. What is
Paul saying to us? 160 pages.

Paperback 978-11936716821 **LB99** $17.99

James the Just Presents Application of Torah

A Messianic Commentary

—Dr. David Friedman

James (Jacob) one of the Epistles written to first century Jewish followers of
Yeshua. Dr. David Friedman, a former Professor of the Israel Bible Institute
has shed new light for Christians from this very important letter.

978-1936716449 **LB82** $14.99

Jude On Faith and the Destructive Influence of Heresy

A Messianic Commentary

—Rabbi Joshua Brumbach

Almost no other canonical book has been as neglected and overlooked as
the Epistle of Jude. This little book may be small, but it has a big message
that is even more relevant today as when it was originally written.

978-1-936716-78-4 **LB97** $14.99

Psalms & Proverbs *Tehillim* תְּהִלִּים-*Mishlei* מִשְׁלֵי
—Translated by Dr. David Stern

Contemplate the power in these words anytime, anywhere: Psalms-*Tehillim* offers uplifting words of praise and gratitude, keeping us focused with the right attitude; Proverbs-*Mishlei* gives us the wisdom for daily living, renewing our minds by leading us to examine our actions, to discern good from evil, and to decide freely to do the good. Makes a wonderful and meaningful gift. Softcover, 224 pages.

978-1936716692	LB90	$9.99

At the Feet of Rabbi Gamaliel
Rabbinic Influence in Paul's Teachings
—David Friedman, Ph.D.

Paul (Shaul) was on the "fast track" to becoming a sage and Sanhedrin judge, describing himself as passionate for the Torah and the traditions of the fathers, typical for an aspiring Pharisee: "…trained at the feet of Gamaliel in every detail of the Torah of our forefathers. I was a zealot for God, as all of you are today" (Acts 22.3, CJB). Did Shaul's teachings reflect Rabbi Gamaliel's instructions? Did Paul continue to value the Torah and Pharisaic tradition? Did Paul create a 'New' Theology? The results of the research within these pages and its conclusion may surprise you. Softcover, 100 pages.

978-1936716753	**LB95**	$8.99

Debranding God *Revealing His True Essence*
—Eduardo Stein

The process of 'debranding' God is to remove all the labels and fads that prompt us to understand him as a supplier and ourselves as the most demanding of customers. Changing our perception of God also changes our perception of ourselves. In knowing who we are in relationship to God, we discover his, and our, true essence. Softcover, 252 pages.

978-1936716708	**LB91**	$16.99

Under the Fig Tree *Messianic Thought Through the Hebrew Calendar*
—Patrick Gabriel Lumbroso

Take a daily devotional journey into the Word of God through the Hebrew Calendar and the Biblical Feasts. Learn deeper meaning of the Scriptures through Hebraic thought. Beautifully written and a source for inspiration to draw closer to Adonai every day. Softcover, 407 pages.

978-1936716760	**LB96**	$25.99

Under the Vine *Messianic Thought Through the Hebrew Calendar*
—Patrick Gabriel Lumbroso

Journey daily through the Hebrew Calendar and Biblical Feasts into the B'rit Hadashah (New Testament) Scriptures as they are put in their rightful context, bringing Judaism alive in it's full beauty. Messianic faith was the motor and what gave substance to Abraham's new beliefs, hope to Job, trust to Isaac, vision to Jacob, resilience to Joseph, courage to David, wisdom to Solomon, knowledge to Daniel, and divine Messianic authority to Yeshua. Softcover, 412 pages.

978-1936716654	**LB87**	$25.99

Come and Worship *Ways to Worship from the Hebrew Scriptures*
—Compiled by Barbara D. Malda

We were created to worship. God has graciously given us many ways to express our praise to him. Each way fits a different situation or moment in life, yet all are intended to bring honor and glory to him. When we believe that he is who he says he is [see *His Names are Wonderful!*] and that his Word is true, worship flows naturally from our hearts to his. Softcover, 128 pages.

978-1936716678   **LB88** $9.99

His Names Are Wonderful
Getting to Know God Through His Hebrew Names
—Elizabeth L. Vander Meulen and Barbara D. Malda

In Hebrew thought, names did more than identify people; they revealed their nature. God's identity is expressed not in one name, but in many. This book will help readers know God better as they uncover the truths in his Hebrew names. 160 pages.

978-1880226308   **LB58** $9.99

The Revolt of Rabbi Morris Cohen
Exploring the Passion & Piety of a Modern-day Pharisee
—Anthony Cardinale

A brilliant school psychologist, Rabbi Morris Cohen went on a one-man strike to protest the systematic mislabeling of slow learning pupils as "Learning Disabled" (to extract special education money from the state). His disciplinary hearing, based on the transcript, is a hilarious read! This effusive, garrulous man with an irresistible sense of humor lost his job, but achieved a major historic victory causing the reform of the billion-dollar special education program. Enter into the mind of an eighth-generation Orthodox rabbi to see how he deals spiritually with the loss of everything, even the love of his children. This modern-day Pharisee discovered a trusted friend in the author (a born again believer in Jesus) with whom he could openly struggle over Rabbinic Judaism as well as the concept of Jesus (Yeshua) as Messiah. Softcover, 320 pages.

978-1936716722   **LB92** $19.99

Stories of Yeshua
—Jim Reimann, Illustrator Julia Filipone-Erez

Children's Bible Storybook with four stories about Yeshua (Jesus). *Yeshua is Born: The Bethlehem Story* based on Lk 1:26-35 & 2:1-20; *Yeshua and Nicodemus in Jerusalem* based on Jn 3:1-16; *Yeshua Loves the Little Children of the World* based on Matthew 18:1–6 & 19:13–15; *Yeshua is Alive-The Empty Tomb in Jerusalem* based on Matthew 26:17-56, Jn 19:16-20:18, Lk 24:50-53. Ages 3-7, Softcover, 48 pages.

978-1936716685   **LB89** $14.99

To the Ends of the Earth – How the First Jewish Followers of Yeshua Transformed the Ancient World
— Dr. Jeffrey Seif

Everyone knows that the first followers of Yeshua were Jews, and that Christianity was very Jewish for the first 50 to 100 years. It's a known fact that there were many congregations made up mostly of Jews, although the false perception today is, that in the second century they disappeared. Dr. Seif reveals the truth of what happened to them and how these early Messianic Jews influenced and transformed the behavior of the known world at that time.

978-1936716463   **LB83** $17.99

Jewish Roots and Foundations of the Scriptures I & II
—John Fischer, Th.D, Ph.D.

An outstanding evangelical leader once said: "There is something shallow about a Christianity that has lost its Jewish roots." A beautiful painting is a careful interweaving of a number of elements. Among other things, there are the background, the foreground and the subject. Discovering the roots of your faith is a little like appreciating the various parts of a painting. In the background is the panorama of preparation and pictures found in the Old Testament. In the foreground is the landscape and light of the first century Jewish setting. All of this is intricately connected with and highlights the subject—which becomes the flowering of all these aspects—the coming of God to earth and what that means for us. Discovering and appreciating your roots in this way broadens, deepens and enriches your faith and your understanding of Scripture. This audio is 32 hours of live class instruction - audio is clear and easy to understand.

9781936716623   **LCD03 / LCD04** $49.99 each

The Gospels in their Jewish Context
—John Fischer, Th.D, Ph.D.

An examination of the Jewish background and nature of the Gospels in their contemporary political, cultural and historical settings, emphasizing each gospel's special literary presentation of Yeshua, and highlighting the cultural and religious contexts necessary for understanding each of the gospels. 32 hours of audio/video instruction on MP3-DVD and pdf of syllabus.

978-1936716241   **LCD01** $49.99

The Epistles from a Jewish Perspective
—John Fischer, Th.D, Ph.D.

An examination of the relationship of Rabbi Shaul (the Apostle Paul) and the Apostles to their Jewish contemporaries and environment; surveys their Jewish practices, teaching, controversy with the religious leaders, and many critical passages, with emphasis on the Jewish nature, content, and background of these letters. 32 hours of audio/video instruction on MP3-DVD and pdf of syllabus.

978-1936716258   **LCD02** $49.99

The Red Heifer *A Jewish Cry for Messiah*
—Anthony Cardinale

Award-winning journalist and playwright Anthony Cardinale has traveled extensively in Israel, and recounts here his interviews with Orthodox rabbis, secular Israelis, and Palestinian Arabs about the current search for a red heifer by Jewish radicals wishing to rebuild the Temple and bring the Messiah. These real-life interviews are interwoven within an engaging and dramatic fictional portrayal of the diverse people of Israel and how they would react should that red heifer be found. Readers will find themselves in the Land, where they can hear learned rabbis and ordinary Israelis talking about the red heifer and dealing with all the related issues and the imminent coming and identity of Messiah.

978-1936716470   LB79 $19.99

The Borough Park Papers
—Multiple Authors

As you read the New Testament, you "overhear" debates first-century Messianic Jews had about critical issues, e.g. Gentiles being "allowed" into the Messianic kingdom (Acts 15). Similarly, you're now invited to "listen in" as leading twenty-first century Messianic Jewish theologians discuss critical issues facing us today. Some ideas may not fit into your previously held pre-suppositions or pre-conceptions. Indeed, you may find some paradigm shifting in your thinking. We want to share the thoughts of these thinkers with you, our family in the Messiah.

Symposium I:
The Gospel and the Jewish People
248 pages

978-1936716593	LB84	$39.95

Symposium II:
The Deity of Messiah and the Mystery of God
211 pages

978-1936716609	LB85	$39.95

Symposium III:
How Jewish Should the Messianic Community Be?

978-1936716616	LB86	$39.95

Passion for Israel: *A Short History of the Evangelical Church's Support of Israel and the Jewish People*
—Dan Juster

History reveals a special commitment of Christians to the Jews as God's still elect people, but the terrible atrocities committed against the Jews by so-called Christians have overshadowed the many good deeds that have been performed. This important history needs to be told to help heal the wounds and to inspire more Christians to stand together in support of Israel.

978-1936716401	**LB78**	$9.99

On The Way to Emmaus: *Searching the Messianic Prophecies*
—Dr. Jacques Doukhan

An outstanding compilation of the most critical Messianic prophecies by a renowned conservative Christian Scholar, drawing on material from the Bible, Rabbinic sources, Dead Sea Scrolls, and more.

978-1936716432	LB80	$14.99

Yeshua *A Guide to the Real Jesus and the Original Church*
—Dr. Ron Moseley

Opens up the history of the Jewish roots of the Christian faith. Illuminates the Jewish background of Yeshua and the Church and never flinches from showing "Jesus was a Jew, who was born, lived, and died, within first century Judaism." Explains idioms in the New Testament. Endorsed by Dr. Brad Young and Dr. Marvin Wilson. 213 pages.

978-1880226681	**LB29**	$12.99

Gateways to Torah *Joining the Ancient Conversation on the Weekly Portion*
—Rabbi Russell Resnik

From before the days of Messiah until today, Jewish people have read from and discussed a prescribed portion of the Pentateuch each week. Now, a Messianic Jewish Rabbi, Russell Resnik, brings another perspective on the Torah, that of a Messianic Jew. 246 pages.

978-1880226889   **LB42** $15.99

Creation to Completion *A Guide to Life's Journey from the Five Books of Moses*
—Rabbi Russell Resnik

Endorsed by Coach Bill McCartney, Founder of Promise Keepers & Road to Jerusalem: "Paul urged Timothy to study the Scriptures (2 Tim. 3:16), advising him to apply its teachings to all aspects of his life. Since there was no New Testament then, this rabbi/apostle was convinced that his disciple would profit from studying the Torah, the Five Books of Moses, and the Old Testament. Now, Rabbi Resnik has written a warm devotional commentary that will help you understand and apply the Law of Moses to your life in a practical way." 256 pages

978-1880226322   **LB61** $14.99

Walk Genesis!   Walk Exodus!   Walk Leviticus!   Walk Numbers!   Walk Deuteronomy!
Messianic Jewish Devotional Commentaries
—Jeffrey Enoch Feinberg, Ph.D.

Using the weekly synagogue readings, Dr. Jeffrey Feinberg has put together some very valuable material in his "Walk" series. Each section includes a short Hebrew lesson (for the non-Hebrew speaker), key concepts, an excellent overview of the portion, and some practical applications. Can be used as a daily devotional as well as a Bible study tool.

Walk Genesis!	238 pages	978-1880226759	**LB34**	$12.99
Walk Exodus!	224 pages	978-1880226872	**LB40**	$12.99
Walk Leviticus!	208 pages	978-1880226926	**LB45**	$12.99
Walk Numbers!	211 pages	978-1880226995	**LB48**	$12.99
Walk Deuteronomy!	231 pages	978-1880226186	**LB51**	$12.99
SPECIAL! Five-book Walk!		5 Book Set **Save $10**	**LK28**	$54.99

Good News According To Matthew
—Dr. Henry Einspruch

English translation with quotations from the Tanakh (Old Testament) capitalized and printed in Hebrew. Helpful notations are included. Lovely black and white illustrations throughout the book. 86 pages.

| | 978-1880226025 | **LB03** | $4.99 |
| Also available in Yiddish. | | **LB02** | $4.99 |

They Loved the Torah *What Yeshua's First Followers Really Thought About the Law*
—Dr. David Friedman

Although many Jews believe that Paul taught against the Law, this book disproves that notion. An excellent case for his premise that all the first followers of the Messiah were not only Torah-observant, but also desired to spread their love for God's entire Word to the gentiles to whom they preached. 144 pages. Endorsed by Dr. David Stern, Ariel Berkowitz, Rabbi Dr. Stuart Dauermann & Dr. John Fischer.

978-1880226940   **LB47** $9.99

The Distortion *2000 Years of Misrepresenting the Relationship Between Jesus the Messiah and the Jewish People*
—Dr. John Fischer & Dr. Patrice Fischer

Did the Jews kill Jesus? Did they really reject him? With the rise of global anti–Semitism, it is important to understand what the Gospels teach about the relationship between Jewish people and their Messiah. 2000 years of distortion have made this difficult. Learn how the distortion began and continues to this day and what you can do to change it. 126 pages. Endorsed by Dr. Ruth Fleischer, Rabbi Russell Resnik, Dr. Daniel C. Juster, Dr. Michael Rydelnik.

978-1880226254   **LB54** $11.99

---

eBooks Now Available!
Versions available for your favorite reader

Visit www.messianicjewish.net for direct links to these readers for each available eBook.

God's Appointed Times *A Practical Guide to Understanding and Celebrating the Biblical Holidays* – **New Edition.**
—Rabbi Barney Kasdan

The Biblical Holy Days teach us about the nature of God and his plan for mankind, and can be a source of God's blessing for all believers–Jews and Gentiles–today. Includes historical background, traditional Jewish observance, New Testament relevance, and prophetic significance, plus music, crafts and holiday recipes. 145 pages.

English	978-1880226353	**LB63**	$12.99
Spanish	978-1880226391	**LB59**	$12.99

God's Appointed Customs *A Messianic Jewish Guide to the Biblical Lifecycle and Lifestyle*
— Rabbi Barney Kasdan

Explains how biblical customs are often the missing key to unlocking the depths of Scripture. Discusses circumcision, the Jewish wedding, and many more customs mentioned in the New Testament. Companion to *God's Appointed Times.* 170 pages.

English	978-1880226636	**LB26**	$12.99
Spanish	978-1880226551	**LB60**	$12.99

Celebrations of the Bible *A Messianic Children's Curriculum*

Did you know that each Old Testament feast or festival finds its fulfillment in the New? They enrich the lives of people who experience and enjoy them. Our popular curriculum for children is in a brand new, user-friendly format. The lay-flat at binding allows you to easily reproduce handouts and worksheets. Celebrations of the Bible has been used by congregations, Sunday schools, ministries, homeschoolers, and individuals to teach children about the biblical festivals. Each of these holidays are presented for Preschool (2-K), Primary (Grades 1-3), Junior (Grades 4-6), and Children's Worship/Special Services. 208 pages.

978-1880226261	**LB55**	$24.99

Passover: *The Key That Unlocks the Book of Revelation*
—Daniel C. Juster, Th.D.

Is there any more enigmatic book of the Bible than Revelation? Controversy concerning its meaning has surrounded it back to the first century. Today, the arguments continue. Yet, Dan Juster has given us the key that unlocks the entire book—the events and circumstances of the Passover/Exodus. By interpreting Revelation through the lens of Exodus, Dan Juster provides a unified overview that helps us read Revelation as it was always meant to be read, as a drama of spiritual conflict, deliverance, and above all, worship. He also shows how this final drama, fulfilled in Messiah, resonates with the Torah and all of God's Word. — Russ Resnik, Executive Director, Union of Messianic Jewish Congregations.

978-1936716210	**LB74**	$10.99

The Messianic Passover Haggadah
Revised and Updated
—Rabbi Barry Rubin and Steffi Rubin.

Guides you through the traditional Passover seder dinner, step-by-step. Not only does this observance remind us of our rescue from Egyptian bondage, but, we remember Messiah's last supper, a Passover seder. The theme of redemption is seen throughout the evening. What's so unique about our Haggadah is the focus on Yeshua (Jesus) the Messiah and his teaching, especially on his last night in the upper room. 36 pages.

English	978-1880226292	**LB57**	$4.99
Spanish	978-1880226599	**LBSP01**	$4.99

The Messianic Passover Seder Preparation Guide
Includes recipes, blessings and songs. 19 pages.

English	978-1880226247	**LB10**	$2.99
Spanish	978-1880226728	**LBSP02**	$2.99

The Sabbath *Entering God's Rest*
—Barry Rubin & Steffi Rubin

Even if you've never celebrated Shabbat before, this book will guide you into the rest God has for all who would enter in—Jews and non-Jews. Contains prayers, music, recipes; in short, everything you need to enjoy the Sabbath, even how to observe havdalah, the closing ceremony of the Sabbath. Also discusses the Saturday or Sunday controversy. 48 pages.

	978-1880226742	**LB32**	$6.99

Havdalah *The Ceremony that Completes the Sabbath*
—Dr. Neal & Jamie Lash

The Sabbath ends with this short, yet equally sweet ceremony called havdalah (separation). This ceremony reminds us to be a light and a sweet fragrance in this world of darkness as we carry the peace, rest, joy and love of the Sabbath into the work week. 28 pages.

	978-1880226605	**LB69**	$4.99

Dedicate and Celebrate!
A Messianic Jewish Guide to Hanukkah
—Barry Rubin & Family

Hanukkah means "dedication" — a theme of significance for Jews and Christians. Discussing its historical background, its modern-day customs, deep meaning for all of God's people, this little book covers all the how-tos! Recipes, music, and prayers for lighting the menorah, all included! 32 pages.

	978-1880226834	**LB36**	$4.99

The Conversation
An Intimate Journal of the Emmaus Encounter
—Judy Salisbury

"Then beginning with Moses and with all the prophets, He explained to them the things concerning Himself in all the Scriptures." Luke 24:27
If you've ever wondered what that conversation must have been like, this captivating book takes you there.

"The Conversation brings to life that famous encounter between the two disciples and our Lord Jesus on the road to Emmaus. While it is based in part on an imaginative reconstruction, it is filled with the throbbing pulse of the excitement of the sensational impact that our Lord's resurrection should have on all of our lives." ~ Dr. Walter Kaiser President Emeritus Gordon-Conwell Theological Seminary. Hardcover 120 pages.

Hardcover	978-1936716173	**LB73**	$14.99
Paperback	978-1936716364	**LB77**	$9.99

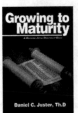

Growing to Maturity
A Messianic Jewish Discipleship Guide
—Daniel C. Juster, Th.D.

This discipleship series presents first steps of understanding and spiritual practice, tailored for the Jewish believer. It's purpose is to aid the believer in living according to Yeshua's will as a disciple, one who has learned the example of his teacher. The course is structured according to recent advances in individualized educational instruction. Discipleship is serious business and the material is geared for serious study and reflection. Each chapter is divided into short sections followed by study questions. 256 pages.

	978-1936716227	**LB75**	$19.99

Growing to Maturity Primer: *A Messianic Jewish*
Discipleship Workbook
—Daniel C. Juster, Th.D.

A basic book of material in question and answer form. Usable by everyone. 60 pages.

	978-0961455507	**TB16**	$7.99

Conveying Our Heritage A Messianic Jewish Guide to Home Practice
—Daniel C. Juster, Th.D. Patricia A. Juster

Throughout history the heritage of faith has been conveyed within the family and the congregation. The first institution in the Bible is the family and only the family can raise children with an adequate appreciation of our faith and heritage. This guide exists to help families learn how to pass on the heritage of spiritual Messianic Jewish life. Softcover, 86 pages

	978-1936716739	**LB93**	$8.99

That They May Be One *A Brief Review of Church Restoration Movements and Their Connection to the Jewish People*
—Daniel Juster, Th.D

Something prophetic and momentous is happening. The Church is finally fully grasping its relationship to Israel and the Jewish people. Author describes the restoration movements in Church history and how they connected to Israel and the Jewish people. Each one contributed in some way—some more, some less—toward the ultimate unity between Jews and Gentiles. Predicted in the Old Testament and fulfilled in the New, Juster believes this plan of God finds its full expression in Messianic Judaism. He may be right. See what you think as you read *That They May Be One*. 100 pages.

978-1880226711   **LB71** $9.99

The Greatest Commandment
How the Sh'ma Leads to More Love in Your Life
—Irene Lipson

"What is the greatest commandment?" Yeshua was asked. His reply—"Hear, O Israel, the Lord our God, the Lord is one, and you are to love Adonai your God with all your heart, with all your soul, with all your understanding, and all your strength." A superb book explaining each word so the meaning can be fully grasped and lived. Endorsed by Elliot Klayman, Susan Perlman, & Robert Stearns. 175 pages.

978-1880226360   **LB65** $12.99

Blessing the King of the Universe
Transforming Your Life Through the Practice of Biblical Praise
—Irene Lipson

Insights into the ancient biblical practice of blessing God are offered clearly and practically. With examples from Scripture and Jewish tradition, this book teaches the biblical formula used by men and women of the Bible, including the Messiah; points to new ways and reasons to praise the Lord; and explains more about the Jewish roots of the faith. Endorsed by Rabbi Barney Kasdan, Dr. Mitch Glaser, & Rabbi Dr. Dan Cohn-Sherbok. 144 pages.

978-1880226797   **LB53** $11.99

You Bring the Bagels, I'll Bring the Gospel
Sharing the Messiah with Your Jewish Neighbor
Revised Edition—Now with Study Questions
—Rabbi Barry Rubin

This "how-to-witness-to-Jewish-people" book is an orderly presentation of everything you need to share the Messiah with a Jewish friend. Includes Messianic prophecies, Jewish objections to believing, sensitivities in your witness, words to avoid. A "must read" for all who care about the Jewish people. Good for individual or group study. Used in Bible schools. Endorsed by Harold A. Sevener, Dr. Walter C. Kaiser, Dr. Erwin J. Kolb and Dr. Arthur F. Glasser. 253 pages.

English	978-1880226650	**LB13**	$12.99
Te Tengo Buenas Noticias	978-0829724103	**OBSP02**	$14.99

Making Eye Contact With God
A Weekly Devotional for Women
—Terri Gillespie

What kind of eyes do you have? Are they downcast and sad? Are they full of God's joy and passion? See yourself through the eyes of God. Using real life anecdotes, combined with scripture, the author reveals God's heart for women everywhere, as she softly speaks of the ways in which women see God. Endorsed by prominent authors: Dr. Angela Hunt, Wanda Dyson and Kathryn Mackel. 247 pages, hardcover.

978-1880226513   **LB68** $19.99

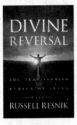

Divine Reversal
The Transforming Ethics of Jesus
—Rabbi Russell Resnik

In the Old Testament, God often reversed the plans of man. Yeshua's ethics continue this theme. Following his path transforms one's life from within, revealing the source of true happiness, forgiveness, reconciliation, fidelity and love. From the introduction, "As a Jewish teacher, Jesus doesn't separate matters of theology from practice. His teaching is consistently practical, ethical, and applicable to real life, even two thousand years after it was originally given." Endorsed by Jonathan Bernis, Dr. Daniel C. Juster, Dr. Jeffrey L. Seif, and Dr Darrell Bock. 206 pages

978-1880226803   **LB72** $12.99

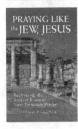

Praying Like the Jew, Jesus
Recovering the Ancient Roots of New Testament Prayer
—Dr. Timothy P. Jones

This eye-opening book reveals the Jewish background of many of Yeshua's prayers. Historical vignettes "transport" you to the times of Yeshua so you can grasp the full meaning of Messiah's prayers. Unique devotional thoughts and meditations, presented in down-to-earth language, provide inspiration for a more meaningful prayer life and help you draw closer to God. Endorsed by Mark Galli, James W. Goll, Rev. Robert Stearns, James F. Strange, and Dr. John Fischer. 144 pages.

978-1880226285   **LB56** $9.99

Growing Your Olive Tree Marriage *A Guide for Couples from Two Traditions*
—David J. Rudolph

One partner is Jewish; the other is Christian. Do they celebrate Hanukkah, Christmas or both? Do they worship in a church or a synagogue? How will the children be raised? This is the first book from a biblical perspective that addresses the concerns of intermarried couples, offering a godly solution. Includes highlights of interviews with intermarried couples. Endorsed by Walter C. Kaiser, Jr., Rabbi Dan Cohn-Sherbok, Jonathan Settel, Dr. Mitchell Glaser & Natalie Sirota. 224 pages.

978-1880226179   **LB50** $12.99

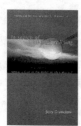

In Search of the Silver Lining *Where is God in the Midst of Life's Storms?*
—Jerry Gramckow

When faced with suffering, what are your choices? Storms have always raged. And people have either perished in their wake or risen above the tempests, shaping history by their responses...new storms are on the horizon. How will we deal with them? How will we shape history or those who follow us? The answer lies in how we view God in the midst of the storms. Endorsed by Joseph C. Aldrich, Ray Beeson, Dr. Daniel Juster. 176 pages.

978-1880226865   **LB39** $10.99

The Voice of the Lord *Messianic Jewish Daily Devotional*
—Edited by David J. Rudolph

Brings insight into the Jewish Scriptures—both Old and New Testaments. Twenty-two prominent Messianic contributors provide practical ways to apply biblical truth. Start your day with this unique resource. Explanatory notes. Perfect companion to the Complete Jewish Bible (see page 2). Endorsed by Edith Schaeffer, Dr. Arthur F. Glaser, Dr. Michael L. Brown, Mitch Glaser and Moishe Rosen. 416 pages.

9781880226704   **LB31** $19.99

Kingdom Relationships *God's Laws for the Community of Faith*
—Dr. Ron Moseley

Dr. Ron Moseley's Yeshua: A Guide to the Real Jesus and the Original Church has taught thousands of people about the Jewishness of not only Yeshua, but of the first followers of the Messiah.
In this work, Moseley focuses on the teaching of Torah -- the Five Books of Moses -- tapping into truths that greatly help modern-day members of the community of faith. 64 pages.

978-1880226841   **LB37** $8.99

Mutual Blessing *Discovering the Ultimate Destiny of Creation*
—Daniel C. Juster

To truly love as God loves is to see the wonder and richness of the distinct differences in all of creation and his natural order of interdependence. This is the way to mutual blessing and the discovery of the ultimate destiny of creation. Learn how to become enriched and blessed as you enrich and bless others and all that is around you! Softcover, 135 pages.

978-1936716746   **LB94** $9.99

Train Up A Child *Successful Parenting For The Next Generation*
—Dr. Daniel L. Switzer

The author, former principal of Ets Chaiyim Messianic Jewish Day School, and father of four, combines solid biblical teaching with Jewish sources on child raising, focusing on the biblical holy days, giving fresh insight into fulfilling the role of parent. 188 pages. Endorsed by Dr. David J. Rudolph, Paul Lieberman, and Dr. David H. Stern.

978-1880226377   **LB64** $12.99

Fire on the Mountain - *Past Renewals, Present Revivals and the Coming Return of Israel*
—Dr. Louis Goldberg

The term "revival" is often used to describe a person or congregation turning to God. Is this something that "just happens," or can it be brought about? Dr. Louis Goldberg, author and former professor of Hebrew and Jewish Studies at Moody Bible Institute, examines real revivals that took place in Bible times and applies them to today. 268 pages.

978-1880226858   **LB38** $15.99

Voices of Messianic Judaism *Confronting Critical Issues Facing a Maturing Movement*
—General Editor Rabbi Dan Cohn-Sherbok

Many of the best minds of the Messianic Jewish movement contributed their thoughts to this collection of 29 substantive articles. Challenging questions are debated: The involvement of Gentiles in Messianic Judaism? How should outreach be accomplished? Liturgy or not? Intermarriage? 256 pages.

978-1880226933   **LB46** $15.99

The Enduring Paradox *Exploratory Essays in Messianic Judaism*
—General Editor Dr. John Fischer

Yeshua and his Jewish followers began a new movement—Messianic Judaism—2,000 years ago. In the 20th century, it was reborn. Now, at the beginning of the 21st century, it is maturing. Twelve essays from top contributors to the theology of this vital movement of God, including: Dr. Walter C. Kaiser, Dr. David H. Stern, and Dr. John Fischer. 196 pages.

978-1880226902   **LB43** $13.99

The World To Come *A Portal to Heaven on Earth*
—Derek Leman

An insightful book, exposing fallacies and false teachings surrounding this extremely important subject... paints a hopeful picture of the future and dispels many non-biblical notions. Intriguing chapters: Magic and Desire, The Vision of the Prophets, Hints of Heaven, Horrors of Hell, The Drama of the Coming Ages. Offers a fresh, but old, perspective on the world to come, as it interacts with the prophets of Israel and the Bible. 110 pages.

978-1880226049   **LB67**   .$9.99

Hebrews Through a Hebrew's Eyes
—Dr. Stuart Sacks

Written to first-century Messianic Jews, this epistle, understood through Jewish eyes, edifies and encourages all. 119 pages. Endorsed by Dr. R.C. Sproul and James M. Boice.

978-1880226612   **LB23** $10.99

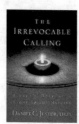

The Irrevocable Calling *Israel's Role As A Light To The Nations*
—Daniel C. Juster, Th.D.

Referring to the chosen-ness of the Jewish people, Paul, the Apostle, wrote "For God's free gifts and his calling are irrevocable" (Rom. 11:29). This messenger to the Gentiles understood the unique calling of his people, Israel. So does Dr. Daniel Juster, President of Tikkun Ministries Int'l. In *The Irrevocable Calling*, he expands Paul's words, showing how Israel was uniquely chosen to bless the world and how these blessings can be enjoyed today. Endorsed by Dr. Jack Hayford, Mike Bickle and Don Finto. 64 pages.

978-1880226346	**LB66**	$8.99

Are There Two Ways of Atonement?
—Dr. Louis Goldberg

Here Dr. Louis Goldberg, long-time professor of Jewish Studies at Moody Bible Institute, exposes the dangerous doctrine of Two-Covenant Theology. 32 pages.

978-1880226056	**LB12**	$ 4.99

Awakening *Articles and Stories About Jews and Yeshua*
—Arranged by Anna Portnov

Articles, testimonies, and stories about Jewish people and their relationship with God, Israel, and the Messiah. Includes the effective tract, "The Most Famous Jew of All." One of our best anthologies for witnessing to Jewish people. Let this book witness for you! Russian version also available. 110 pages.

English	978-1880226094	**LB15**	$ 6.99
Russian	978-1880226018	**LB14**	$ 6.99

The Unpromised Land *The Struggle of Messianic Jews Gary and Shirley Beresford*
—Linda Alexander

They felt God calling them to live in Israel, the Promised Land. Wanting nothing more than to live quietly and grow old together in the country of refuge for all Jewish people, little did they suspect what events would follow to try their faith. The fight to make *aliyah*, to claim their rightful inheritance in the Promised Land, became a battle waged not only for themselves, but also for Messianic Jews all over the world that wish to return to the Jewish homeland. Here is the true saga of the Beresford's journey to the land of their forefathers. 216 pages.

978-1880226568	**LB19**	$ 9.99

Death of Messiah *Twenty fascinating articles that address a subject of grief, hope, and ultimate triumph.*
—Edited by Kai Kjaer-Hansen

This compilation, written by well-known Jewish believers, addresses the issue of Messiah and offers proof that Yeshua—the true Messiah—not only died, but also was resurrected! 160 pages.

978-1880226582   **LB20** $ 8.99

Beloved Dissident *(A Novel)*
—Laurel West

A gripping story of human relationships, passionate love, faith, and spiritual testing. Set in the world of high finance, intrigue, and international terrorism, the lives of David, Jonathan, and Leah intermingle on many levels--especially their relationships with one another and with God. As the two men tangle with each other in a rising whirlwind of excitement and danger, each hopes to win the fight for Leah's love. One of these rivals will move Leah to a level of commitment and love she has never imagined--or dared to dream. Whom will she choose? 256 pages.

978-1880226766   **LB33** $ 9.99

Sudden Terror
—Dr. David Friedman

Exposes the hidden agenda of militant Islam. The author, a former member of the Israel Defense Forces, provides eye-opening information needed in today's dangerous world.

Dr. David Friedman recounts his experiences confronting terrorism; analyzes the biblical roots of the conflict between Israel and Islam; provides an overview of early Islam; demonstrates how the United States and Israel are bound together by a common enemy; and shows how to cope with terrorism and conquer fear. The culmination of many years of research and personal experiences. This expose will prepare you for what's to come! 160 pages.

978-1880226155   **LB49** $ 9.99

It is Good! *Growing Up in a Messianic Family*
—Steffi Rubin

Growing up in a Messianic Jewish family. Meet Tovah! Tovah (Hebrew for "Good") is growing up in a Messianic Jewish home, learning the meaning of God's special days. Ideal for young children, it teaches the biblical holidays and celebrates faith in Yeshua. 32 pages to read & color.

978-1880226063   **LB11** $ 4.99